MIXED
BLESSING

MIXED
BLESSING

Doris McMillon
with Michele Sherman

St. Martin's Press
New York

Design by Doris Borowsky

Library of Congress Cataloging in Publication Data

McMillon, Doris.
    Mixed blessing.

    1. McMillon, Doris.   2. Adoptees—United States—
Biography.   3. Birthparents—United States—Identifi-
cation.   I. Sherman, Michele.   II. Title.
HV874.82.M37A36   1985   362.8   85-11752
ISBN 0-312-53527-9

First Edition

10 9 8 7 6 5 4 3 2 1

To my mom, Louise, for driving me to succeed, with all the emotions—happy and sad, bitter and sweet—that remembering brings

—Doris

In memory of my mom, Vivian Rothberg, with love.

—Michele

CONTENTS

1

ACORNS

ONE

I ALWAYS KNEW I'D find my natural mother, even before I knew her name. Before Dad showed me the headless photo. Before Louise, in one of her consuming rages, gave too much away.

Before Wilhelm Shuster turned my dreams into half-believed nightmares; but that remains a mystery. Wilhelm's motives, after all this time, go unexplained.

Before any of my own growing up was done, starting from that never-to-be-forgotten day of the naturalization ceremony, there was always the compulsion of the fantasy. . . .

"It's called 'naturalization,'" Daddy said. "It's like a little ceremony."

The living room was dim. It was a gray and cloudy day, and I felt suddenly uncertain. Vulnerable.

Daddy glanced over to Mom, who was moving restlessly back and forth and muttering something.

"I know," said Daddy, inspired. "Let's make it a whole special day, to celebrate. What can we do special after the ceremony, Louise?"

His arm slipped around my waist, and we both looked expectantly at Mom. She stopped her pacing then and studied us blankly, me standing a little stiff and bewildered over all this serious stuff, and Daddy down at my level, crouched on the rug.

I was five years old.

If I'd felt anything at all when Daddy mentioned "naturalization," it was nothing more than confusion over something I'd never heard before. But with Mom staring so darkly and the silence drawing out so thick, I started being frightened. She looked so queer, gone inside herself. Apart from Daddy and me, behind a barrier.

"Just explain to Doris, Mac," she finally commanded him.

Daddy patted me absentmindedly.

I was starting to feel very bad by now, all this long silence making knots inside me. It occurred to me I could easily go to my neighbor, Joey, who was already six, and whose daddy was in the air force, like my daddy. I could ask Joey all about this naturalization thing, since he must already have been naturalized.

But Dad turned me toward him and took my face between his hands.

"Naturalization's something that happens when you become a citizen of the United States," he told me, smiling.

I didn't understand that at all. This *was* the United States, and I was in it. Didn't that make me a citizen?

"And you have to 'become' a citizen because you weren't born here. You were born in Germany."

Well, I knew that, of course. Mom and Dad talked about

4

old times, and sometimes I listened; I knew I was born in Germany.

But Mom sighed, a hard, heavy sigh from behind, and the room was suddenly a threatening place, even grayer and darker than it had been before. Mom crossed the room and pulled me around to look her in the eye. She took a sudden sharp breath, then talked so fast I could barely make out the words.

"You have to be naturalized because your mother wasn't an American." She blurted it, so sudden and fierce and frightening.

"She was foreign," Mom said, her voice rising a little, too loud and hard. "You were adopted from that foreign woman, and being adopted means you're not our own child."

Dad stood, moving me off to the right.

"Louise . . ."

She shot her hand out, sideways, as if that would silence him, pulling herself ramrod stiff.

"It's best to tell the truth," she snapped, her voice grim. "You start with lies, it only seems like self-indulgence later on when they come back to tie you all up in your own deceit."

There was a small silence.

"After all," she said reasonably enough, "the truth won't just vanish, will it?"

The truth, whatever that was, must have been truly terrible to have made my stomach so tight and hurting. It wasn't the words that meant anything at all to a five-year-old, only the atmosphere. Mom sounded different than she'd ever sounded before, but I couldn't understand the change. And Dad just looked furious and didn't say anything, as if he was afraid anything he said would make things worse.

5

Mom was still staring at me. "Doris," she said, then put her hand to her lips and fell silent as well.

It was suddenly the most important thing in my world to be alone. But Mom came across to me where I wavered by the door, and bent a little, looking at me, then tentatively touched my hair. Her hand was steady, but her face scared me, because I didn't know it anymore. Her expression was so strange. I couldn't go to her for comfort or the answers to important questions.

"Doris," she repeated, "you're adopted, Doris. You can't run away from the truth. You have to face truth, Doris, all through life, and make the best of it you can, no matter how poorly things start out.

"You're adopted, and that means I didn't carry you in my own body. Some other woman did. And that other woman," she added, "was German, not American, which means you're a German, too, not an American like Daddy and me, and until you're formally naturalized in this ceremony, you're just a foreigner, not a real American citizen.

"That's all you have to know right now," she decided, flatly, and turned her back on me.

I had no comprehension at all as to what had just happened. There was nothing to explain how I could have started the day normally, in a five-year-old haze centered mostly on my own pleasure, and then suddenly come to this abyss of fear and uncertainty. Dad stood looking first at Mom, then at me, and I thought if there was no reason to be scared, he'd say something comforting, wouldn't he?

I slipped from the room, and Dad started talking to Mom, softly; I didn't try to hear. I hurried to my tiny bedroom and shut the door, then embarked on my first single-minded rationalization—a defense I'd carry with me into fantasy over the next twenty-five years.

Mom hadn't really meant there was anything *wrong*. She hadn't *said* there was anything wrong, had she? I was just being silly, worrying like that, not understanding simple things. But now, lying on my bed, holding my soft doll tight, I could go back over it all and not be so afraid.

I was born in Germany. There was nothing to fear in that; Dad was in the air force and we moved around a lot. And obviously people who kept moving around were always being foreign and needing to be naturalized to keep them American citizens. It made perfect sense now that I was alone, and I couldn't figure out why I'd felt so worried, back in the living room, faced with Dad and Mom.

As for the rest, that part about some other woman and about being carried in somebody's body—that wasn't something I could possibly comprehend. I had no understanding at age five of where babies came from. So the idea that parents might not be your own parents really didn't make sense, and I shelved it.

As for Mom being upset . . . ? Well, she just *was*. She probably didn't feel good, and even when she did, I never really understood Mom. She wasn't easy, like Daddy. Daddy played with me and told me stories and was always the same person. Mom, on any given day, was always a puzzle. . . .

Twenty-five years later, I still wouldn't understand Mom, but the level of bewilderment would be quite different.

TWO

We moved around so much, post to post. And after I was formally naturalized, Mom used the word "adoption" often. Maybe she was trying to make it a natural part of life, something that wouldn't come to have unfamiliar, threatening connotations.

But it encouraged me to ask questions. And I learned early on that Mom wouldn't deal with these questions.

"But why," I said one day, "didn't *you* have me?"

Mom was making dinner and her back was turned, her hands busy over pots and pans on the stove. We'd been talking about clothes—she loved to talk about clothes; she dressed me up like a high-fashion doll and showed me off to everyone. The atmosphere in the kitchen was warm and comfortable, which encouraged me to ask this all-important question.

After a bit, not turning, she spoke.

8

"Looking ahead is everything, Doris. Looking back is futile."

I was only six years old, so looking back didn't encompass a lot, especially with the beginning of my life shrouded in mystery.

"Was I born in a hospital in Germany?" I asked curiously, hoping to learn great truths by just finding the right entry questions.

"You were born in a hospital," Mom admitted, stirring the vegetables.

I sighed, relieved, for I had some half-formed notion by this time that if you were born in a hospital, no "woman's body" was involved in the procedure.

Mom half-turned. If she'd left it like that, I might have been content for a little while, until my increasing maturity taught me better questions. But she seemed almost driven to push the matter into other paths. Her voice was dogged when she continued.

"You were born in a hospital in Munich, and it must have been a terrible ordeal for that woman. Not having a husband, knowing what the nurses and doctors would all think . . ." Her shoulders looked drawn together and tight, hunched against me or her own angry thoughts.

I was confused about this business of no husband. And here was that other woman cropping up again, and I tended to worry over her.

"A white woman having a black child in Germany, so soon after the war," Mom mused, then snorted contemptuously.

New thoughts, these. Unsettling things. This "other woman" so mysteriously connected to myself was white? And also, she wasn't married, which meant there was no

Daddy even if *she* was a Mommy, yet she'd had a baby—or wasn't that right?

But there I drew a total blank. All I knew for sure was that Mom was once more distant and angry, as she always became when I asked her about my adoption. And the result of all this was that I still didn't know what being adopted really meant.

Mom loved to buy me pretty clothes and dress me up. We always had lots of company, no matter where Daddy was stationed, so there was plenty of opportunity for little fashion shows.

As I turned seven, then eight, my memories of daily events grew clearer, and the people around me took on sharper colors and lines. I also came to categorize different tour-of-duty locations by vivid memories of the events happening at these times. Therefore, France, at age seven and eight, was the location of the milk with wax chunks and the episode that followed.

Mom and I had had one of our shopping trips two days before. I had so many new clothes, so endlessly bought, then disposed of, that I never really had time to consider any of them my own. I was always modeling all the new dresses and skirts and blouses she bought.

The night of the milk incident, I had on a filmy pink and white dress. There were white shoes and a little bag to match. I knew I looked nice, but I didn't let myself feel strongly for the outfit. It would follow all its predecessors to the thrift shop when I'd worn it two or three times and Mom decided it was used enough to buy me something else.

I wasn't old enough then to worry over money, to realize we would have to be rich to support my transient wardrobe. I didn't know how desperate Dad got over the bills,

10

or that there simply wasn't enough money available for him to bow to Louise's endless whims.

All I knew was what I wanted to believe. Mom spent all that time shopping for my clothes because she loved me to look nice. Hadn't she told me over and over again that she didn't mind how many sacrifices she had to make, she wanted the best for me always? That she wanted me to know how lucky I was, having been adopted by parents who put their child first, above their own needs? That she wanted me always to remember how much she'd given me when she hadn't had to take me at all.

She bought for me, gave to me—she loved me.

Well, the house was bright and cheerful for our company, and I preened and posed as my mother wished, and everybody made appropriate appreciative comments.

I went to Mom in the kitchen just before dinner, warmed by the attention I'd received. I wanted to hug her and tell her how much I loved her for giving me all this. She was sprinkling sugar on sliced peaches to put in the refrigerator and get nice and syrupy. I came up behind her and put my arms around her and rubbed my cheek against her waist.

She put down the spoon and half-turned in my clasp, her hand touching my hair lightly. Then she gave me a little push, impatient, and adjusted her apron.

"I have to get this done, Doris," she said, without expression. "What do you want?"

My words of love stuck quite suddenly in my throat. She'd been smiling and laughing with the company just minutes before, but now there was no sign of pleasure on her face at all.

"I—I wanted to thank you," I said lamely. "For my dress."

I stood awkwardly, trying to meet her eyes and failing; they bored through me with a dead, black glare.

11

"I buy you lots of nice dresses, don't I, Doris?" she asked coldly.

I nodded dumbly, not understanding what I'd said or done to make her mad.

"I don't remember you ever going out of your way to thank me before for all I do for you," she said. "So why bother now? Or do you just think everybody will hear you and say what a nice child you are and what nice manners you have?"

I stared at her, my heart starting to thud sickeningly in my chest. She was glaring at me, growing angrier by the second, and I truly couldn't understand why.

"Never a sign of *honest* thanks," she said more loudly. "You still don't know how lucky you are. How easily we could have left you with that whore . . ."

I escaped from the kitchen, shaken. There was no place I could go. Mom announced dinner seconds later, and we all sat down around the table. The company didn't seem to notice the change in the atmosphere, but Daddy did; he stared at Mom, then at me, and lifted his eyebrow. But Mom chose that minute to put a glass of milk at my place, and the whole world stopped for me.

The glass was high and fat, a genuine pitcher glass of thick white milk, filled to the brim. I sat and stared at this offering and felt sick. Telling me to drink milk was telling me to die; that wasn't any secret. The milk here in France always had big wax chunks inside, floating around, hitting my lip, and I couldn't drink a glass without gagging and losing my dinner.

"Drink the milk," Mom said matter-of-factly.

Nothing existed in the world but my milk and Mom and me. All the company must have gone on eating; I didn't see them or hear them.

"I can't," I whispered, the room blurring through tears, while my heart started thudding in the awful way it did

12

these days when I knew something nasty and degrading was about to happen to me. These terrible, inexplicable times were happening more and more frequently. Mom would go from warm and giving to cold and punishing without warning. She said I was a disappointment, that she had to straighten me out or my bad blood would someday destroy me.

"Of course you can drink it." Mom managed to sound really surprised. "That milk's healthy, why else would I give you all that? If you didn't want any milk, why didn't you say something before I poured it?" Her voice grew coldly resentful. "Wasting good food, wasteful, ungrateful child, I know what to do to correct that, Doris, *I* know what to do about it!"

We might have been truly alone; that's how little the company suddenly mattered. She went tramping away to return with the heavy extension cord from the television. I was up out of my chair before she'd cleared the doorway, and she whipped me all around the room, catching me on the leg a terrible whack, other places, too, while I kept choking in my throat with the effort not to make a sound—for some reason it seemed I'd disgrace myself more if I screamed and howled.

Dad had come to his feet, between me and Mom, and I took the chance to run from the room and huddle on my bed, crumpling my brand-new dress. My little white bag had fallen on the floor, and I didn't bother to retrieve it. I knew what Mom would be telling everybody: how Dad was too lenient; how disrespectful I was, and how wasteful and ungrateful. I suppose they all sympathized with her rotten bad luck, having a husband who wouldn't support her in the discipline of their child, and a child who had turned out so awful.

So France was milk and thick wax chunks and other things, too, none of them happy tourist memories.

13

We came home to the States in 1961, to Westover Air Force Base at Indian Orchard, Massachusetts, and Indian Orchard became home to fierce, raging battles and escalating weird behavior on the part of my mother.

I was older now. Nine. I knew, vaguely, where babies came from. This created a whole new generation of unsettling questions in my mind about the difference between me—an adopted child—and someone not adopted. I'd learned the hard way that I couldn't talk about this to my mother, so I tried to express my confusion and growing fears of rejection to Dad.

"But Mom said I was somebody else's baby," I remember protesting when he said my questions would have to wait until I was grown up. "She said that already, so why can't I know whose baby I really am?"

He looked tired. "Why does it matter, Doris? You're our little girl now, and you almost always have been." He regarded me for a long minute in silence.

"When you're a grown woman, and if this is still so important to you as it seems to be now, you can find your own answers to things, Doris, without hurting other people. Your mother feels very strongly about this, that's why she gets so upset when you nag at her."

"But why does she feel that way?" I persisted, with the dogged insensitivity of a nine-year-old.

He considered this seriously before answering. "I think," he said, "because she loves you so very much that she can't bear to think of a time when you weren't *her* daughter."

But I'd already started doubting she loved me at all, and that was the crux of the problem. My natural curiosity about being adopted, once I started to understand what that meant, might have itched and annoyed me until I found some solid answers, but it was Mom's furious, debasing attitude that turned normal curiosity to obsession.

14

I reasoned that there had to be something in my past or something just in me that was unlovable. Something I hadn't been able to change or control, which kept Mom from loving me. Because surely she'd *wanted* to love me. Look at all she'd done for me. The tremendous sacrifice she'd made, just adopting me.

That's what she told me.

Life wasn't calm, but it was our norm. It didn't occur to me then, but I guess she drove Dad crazy. I was too young to notice. My main concern was for myself. Everything else was secondary. I knew she'd periodically pack up all his clothes and put them in a suitcase and put it on the step outside. I knew she'd thrown his things from a window more than once. That she'd even hidden his shirts, one morning, out in the garbage. I'd heard her on the phone one day when Dad had left for work. Talking to his superior, saying that Dad always beat her. This horrified me. I knew it was a lie and I hadn't known, until then, that Mom lied about anything.

But none of that had the immediacy that comes with being the focus. Not until the night Dad came home early and found Mom with a friend, talking in the basement. The friend was a serviceman, too, and Dad wasn't happy. When Mom and he were finally alone, a real battle started. And when I tried to grab Dad's arm, afraid that this time he'd really hit Mom, he swung, she ducked, and I bought the punch. The truly amazing quantity of blood that spouted from my nose, covering my shirt, at least had the benefit of stopping that argument.

So Indian Orchard was accusations and beginning violence. A growing determination on my part to understand the meaning of my adoption. If Mom hadn't carried me inside her, then who had, and was that other woman my *real* mother? And if she was, why had Mom and Dad taken me from her?

Dad started thinking, about this time, of entering the ministry. Mom went into one of her utter rages and defied him and taunted him without mercy. She even went so far as to drag me to Catholic services, though she was a Baptist, like Dad, just to show him how much she disdained him for wanting to make her something she wouldn't tolerate—the wife of a Baptist minister.

And finally, as if all this uncertainty wasn't enough, there was one more surprising development.

One night the phone rang, and Dad answered. He put Mom on, and seconds later she'd gone stiff and sick-looking. I was sent abruptly to my room, but the walls were too thin for secrets. Besides, Mom and Dad got louder and louder as they argued, so I really couldn't help hearing. Somebody named Caroline wanted to come and live with us.

"Of course she can come if you want her, Louise," Dad said impatiently. "She *is* your daughter."

"I don't want her," my mother said grimly, but that one word had fastened inside my head.

Her daughter? *I* was her daughter.

"She'll have to learn to cope with whatever her situation is now," Mom said hotly. "If she wanted to come be with me so much, she could have called anytime before."

"She was a little young before," Dad said reasonably.

"She's always known I was her *real* mother." Mom's voice was rising steadily.

Her *real* mother?

"She's also known you gave her up because you weren't married when you had her." Dad unwisely persisted in trying to reason with her.

Wasn't married? Mom had a daughter before she married Daddy? Before they came to Germany and took me away from the mother who would call me *her* real daughter?

16

"That part of my life's over now," Mom said angrily. "I can't have any more children of my own, and I don't want to think about Caroline."

Couldn't. Have children of her own. So she'd settled for adoption.

"Well, that's fine then, if it's what you want. After all, we do have our own little girl," Dad said quietly. "We could hardly have done better ourselves."

But the love in his voice passed over my head. I was fixated on one thought only. Someone named Caroline was my mom's real child, the child she'd wanted. And I was just a poor substitute. A replacement for Caroline.

We moved to Offutt Air Force Base, in Omaha, Nebraska, in February 1964. Omaha was broken eyeglasses and headless photographs and Mom threatening either to leave Dad or to kill him.

I'd lost my glasses on the school playground, and I knew I'd be better off dead than creeping on home to confess it. Sure enough, Mom heard my terrified, mumbled apology, then dragged me back to the schoolyard.

"I'm not surprised, Doris," she snapped. "Blood always tells, but that can be corrected and I'll make sure you don't turn out like that whore who gave birth to you."

I was old enough now to understand what a whore was, but I really couldn't relate it to myself or to my natural mother somewhere in Germany. How could Mom consider anyone a whore just for having a child without being married? Hadn't Mom done the same, having Caroline? And if Mom meant my natural mother was a *prostitute* . . . Well, that was something I couldn't deal with.

My most immediate concern that afternoon wasn't my natural mother or a girl named Caroline, who, it had finally occurred to me, must be some kind of sister, but something

17

much more mundane—those missing eyeglasses Mom had sacrificed good money to buy for me.

All the way back to the schoolyard, she kept shaking me hard and muttering about disease and whores and filth. The blood was thudding and drumming in my ears and even finding the glasses over by the fence didn't help; one of the earpieces was missing.

I was sent to bed early, without supper, with the dread of being sure this episode wasn't over. Sure enough, the next morning, very early, Mom shook me from sleep. It was still dark outside. I didn't know what time it could be.

"I want you out of this house," she said, her voice choking in her throat. "I don't want you anymore. Your own mother didn't want you, she threw you out; well, she was smart, wasn't she? I've given you all I have, I've sacrificed my best years and money besides, and you're nothing, you'll always be nothing, it's in your blood.

"Get dressed," she growled, her face inches from my own, "and get out. Quick before I kill you!"

My own mother hadn't wanted me? Had thrown me out? I wanted to scream at her not to say these things, that the words cut me with an agony I'd never before experienced, not ever, not even in the midst of my worst punishments. How could she possibly fail to see that saying these things was the worst wounding she could do to me?

My natural mother hadn't wanted me. My adoptive mother didn't want me. There must be something desperately wrong with me.

My red plaid lunchbox was standing next to the front door when I stumbled, shaking and stunned, down the stairs. My jeans were half-zipped; my shirt was half-buttoned; I was dizzy with panic and the remnants of sleep. Mom picked up my lunchbox and shoved it under my arm and opened the door and threw me out on the stoop. Locked the storm door. Closed and locked the inside door.

18

Pulled all the blinds shut all around the house, as if for a death.

I stood for a long time and stared at the house. Then I sat on the stoop, hugging my lunchbox in my lap. After a long while, I opened it. Inside were a baloney sandwich, an apple, and some carrot sticks. I stared at these things, with the tears running down my cheeks and dropping off my chin. Closed the lid and clutched the box to my chest, which ached terribly. Rocked then, and rocked and rocked and rocked until finally I opened the lid again and started eating the carrot sticks. Then I ate the baloney sandwich and the sky got lighter and it stayed very quiet all along the street.

When every crumb of the sandwich was gone, I closed my lunchbox and put it carefully on the step, then stood, stiff and sick, and turned to the door and laid both hands on the screen.

"Mommy?" My voice was a hoarse whisper. "Mommy!" I pounded then, frantically, with both fists on the screen.

"Please let me come home, Mommy! I'll be a better girl. I promise. I'll be whatever you want me to be!"

After a long while, she let me in.

That night Dad came to my room. I'd been lying on the bed, staring at the ceiling and wishing I was dead, hating Mom for hating *me* and hating Dad for never being able to change anything.

Dad slipped a snapshot into my hand. I stared at it dully, without much curiosity. It was a picture of a baby, a tiny black girl, in the lap of a woman whose face I couldn't see for the simple reason that the part of the picture with the woman's head had been cut off by the photographer. This faceless woman's arms were tight around the child, and there was a sense of desperation in her clutch that wasn't just my overactive imagination.

"That's you with your real mother," Dad whispered.

"The mother who had you, then had to give you up for adoption when I was stationed in Germany. I thought maybe it would help. . . ." He hesitated, then rubbed his palm over his mouth.

"Well now, Doris, her name was Josefine."

He stared at me for a long second, squinting as if he had a headache, not sure I was taking in what he was imparting.

"She was a beautiful girl," he said gently, his hand on my shoulder, staring at the picture which told me so little.

"White. A lovely woman. A decent woman," he stressed. "She worked in an office, as a secretary.

"She had you, but she wasn't married so she had to give you up. After all, you were a black child and this was Germany, right after the war, and things were very very bad for black people in Germany.

"She wanted the best possible life for you, Doris, and when she learned that Louise and I were wanting to adopt a baby, well—" he looked back to a time I would have given a lot to see—"we just sort of got together and that's how you came to be adopted.

"And that's all there is to tell," he said flatly. "So stop asking Louise about your natural mother, and stop expecting her to act rational about things that only upset her.

"And try to understand a little," he said. "You're growing up. You're old enough to try to have compassion for other people and not to be totally self-centered like little kids tend to be."

But here he stopped. He looked helpless and uneasy.

"Your mother—Louise—she's afraid."

I didn't believe him. My mother wasn't afraid of anything.

Then he took the picture back, firmly.

"Afraid," he repeated, rising. "Of losing things."

When he'd gone, I lay thinking about what he'd said. Rolling the name Josefine around and around inside my head. Until now, my dreams of my "real" mother were purest mist, touching on nothing solid because I had nothing definite to deal with. I tried, then, to feel a sense of familiarity toward her name. Josefine. I kept it moving around and around in my head. I told myself I felt comforted—that was apparently what Dad wanted me to feel.

But all the picture and the name really accomplished was to fill me with the gnawing certainty that there were other pictures, more revealing ones, somewhere in the house. Other hidden *things* to explain the mysteries of my past life. I now wondered what else there was to know. What solid facts about my past existed, close at hand, that would make me feel more like a complete, deserving person.

That's when I knew I'd *have* to find out. I didn't know how, but that didn't matter; only the resolution to *do* it counted. What Dad had said about my natural mother and how pretty and nice she was should have soothed me, but it didn't. Instead, I suddenly felt I couldn't trust him on this subject—what he told me was too totally different from what Mom had always said.

That left it solely up to me to ferret out the truth: Where exactly *was* I born? Who were my natural parents—not just my mother, but my father too? What were they like with each other, were they in love, were they very young . . . ? I needed some romance to see me through. Because the ultimate question would remain until I faced them both and knew the truth.

My stomach clenched cold just thinking it: Why had they really given me up?

THREE

I WAS TWELVE WHEN real crisis struck in my adoptive family. Not that the atmosphere before that time had fostered security; Mom had filled the intervening years with bitter allusions to Josefine and my adoption, while hounding Dad about his work, his habits, his fidelity—everything.

I'd begun to wonder about the home lives of the other kids at school. They all moaned and groaned so much—were any of them, just possibly, adopted, too? Or wasn't that even a factor in the problems we all experienced? Was it a natural phenomenon for a daughter to get along better with her father, while clashing miserably with her mother?

Our favorite pastime at that age was sharing grievances about our parents. We were universally misunderstood; our parents were mean with allowances and slavedrivers in terms of the chores they expected us to do.

We spent endless hours touching on, then shying away from, mention of our mothers. But from the bits and pieces

22

we all managed to drop, a picture emerged of women vacillating between angels and devils. A mother was a cosy friend, curled up at her daughter's bedside, gossiping and sharing feminine secrets. She was likewise a catty bitch, remote and scary, herself entered into that world fantasized about by preadolescent girls: womanhood.

One and all, our mothers showed both sides of the coin, severely opposing personalities. What I didn't get from these discussions was any sense of *degree,* and that made it impossible for me to know what "normal" was between a mother and a daughter.

Because, on the surface, wasn't my situation pretty much the same? Louise talked to me about men a lot, though her conversation was often bawdy enough to shock me. And she'd always cared about my looks and clothes. Our shopping trips together were the ultimate in "just us girls."

And I suppose I could see that her withdrawal at any mention of Josefine was jealousy. After all, women didn't like other women. That was the oldest "truth" in the book, wasn't it?

As for the rest—the violence of her mood swings, her fury at Dad over everything and nothing—these things embarrassed and upset me and I never mentioned them.

I needed to be older and a lot wiser than I was at twelve to be able to understand that while some of my problems with Louise were those faced by many mothers and daughters, other factors came into our particular picture, and these factors had little to do, personally, with me or my adoption.

Some of this was evident when she turned the full force of her misery and anger toward Dad, that spring I was twelve, in Omaha. She was furious with his growing determination to enter the ministry. She was also outraged by his military placement and kept nagging him to try to get a transfer elsewhere. She loathed Omaha, Nebraska.

23

I was an unwilling witness to battles without end—the rupturing of all lifelines.

"You *fool!* You ignorant ass fool! Pullin' that horseshit, you *must* be crazy, I see it *all* now!"

Mom. Louise Evelyn.

I was huddled in the bathroom at the top of the stairs, waiting for the inevitable second when I'd get tossed into the middle of this latest battle between my mom and my dad.

"I put up with your notions, I put up with your habits, I put up with this *piss-hole* you stuck us all down in, but *this* does it! *This* is the end! Do you hear me, you son of a bitch?"

She could be such a lady, quiet and refined with strangers, and the plunge to this level of outrage and cursing still shocked me, though it shouldn't have. It was my most immediate reality.

"We're leaving Omaha. We're *leaving* Omaha. Now. Today. Before another night passes. If you don't get a transfer out of here, we'll leave in three pine boxes!"

There was a thud, then some muffled sounds, like growling voices, and I figured Mom was trying to choke Dad as I'd seen her do not long ago when she was furious. Of course, nothing before had ever been this bad. This morning, at breakfast, Dad had announced his final decision. He was definitely going to become a Baptist minister like *his* father before him.

I'd crept from the table to hide in the bathroom. It was the only room in the house, except their own, where I could shoot the lock—my bedroom was defenseless. Not that the bathroom lock meant anything real. Mom had never busted it in, but that was only because I was so sure she'd kill me if I left it locked that I always opened up for her the second she ordered me out.

24

I was going to be late for school, again, and the class play tryouts. I'd dearly *wanted* to make those tryouts.

I heard a distant and mysterious *thud thud thud,* didn't know what it was, had no time to make things up.

"Doris!"

"Smart" would have been leaving the house. "Stupid" was hiding in the bathroom where Mom was sure to look first.

"Doris! Get down here! Fast!"

I strained for any evidence my dad was still around, but only silence followed that command.

"Please," I ventured, and my voice came out too high and thin through the door. "Please, Mommy, don't hit me."

"Stop whining," she roared, "and get yourself down here. We're leaving Omaha. Do you hear me? We're leaving Omaha and you get your ass down those steps fast! Do you *hear* me?"

Everybody on the street must have heard her by now. It was late spring; all the house windows were open, and our business was everybody's business. Dad should have re-thought his announcement if he wanted any peace. No *way* was my mom ever going to be stifled, married to a Baptist minister! Hadn't she already said so in no uncertain terms when he'd told her he was considering it? Hadn't she even gone so far as to take me to Catholic services, to keep me from falling under his influence?

"You hear me, fool?" Her voice was further away, and I crept from the bathroom, inching down the steps, shuddering with fright, wondering why I hadn't used the toilet all that time I was cowering alongside it. Mom always had that effect on me now. She scared me shitless.

The stairs were clear. The front door was straight down the steps, the living room off to the right as I crouched on the bottom tread. If I could make my feet move a little bit faster, if the door wasn't locked—it always stuck, the

25

lock—if I was quick enough, didn't look back at horrors, didn't stop for my books or my lunchbox . . .

"You!" It was a sharp hiss, and it turned me all the way around. There stood the only mother I'd ever known, in the middle of the living room, gripping a heavy-handled hammer in her big right fist and something I couldn't see in her left. I quickly looked away from the hammer, stopped breathing and thinking too, paralyzed.

"We're leaving Nebraska," Mom said, voice hot on the edge of hysteria. "We're *leaving* Nebraska!" This on a rising screech. "I'm not staying here another night. But first . . ."

She turned and tramped back toward the dining room, and I heard again that smashing *thud thud thud*. Again I didn't take my chance and run. Curiosity, my downfall, led me after her.

Sure enough, there was Mom, demolishing her new dining room table. She'd saved and saved; we'd only had it two months. She'd polished it daily; she was proud of that table; it was her showpiece, like me, for company.

Wood screeched, then cracked. She finally looked up. Her eyes were blank, staring past me and through me, not focusing on my real self. The hammer was still gripped in her right hand, and in her left . . . ?

Suddenly I couldn't swallow. Even my breath stopped. There was a kitchen knife in her left hand, not the kind we used to cut up butter and bread, the kind we used to hack up tough stuff.

I ran. Not for the front door. That seemed too straight a shot. I'd seen Mom take aim at Dad when he'd come in late one night. Instead I turned and hurled myself back up the steps, beelining it toward the false safety of the bathroom, when I heard my mother's voice, from just behind. . . . Doom . . .

"I'll *kill* you!"

Then the whisper of air and a whack! It froze me there,

by the bathroom door, and turned my head without my help. The knife quivered in the wood, embedded in the doorframe, inches from my left cheek.

Dad always said Mom was a whiz with a blade, and he didn't mean only carving up chops.

She was up on the landing then and whirling me around, dragging me back down those steps, punching me, for good measure, wherever she could hurt, then tossing me into the front door, cursing, yanking me back just long enough to pull it wide and shove me out.

Dad was gone. He'd made his escape when he could. I doubt he'd imagined I was still in the house; he would have given me credit for more common sense than that. Mom, her face contorted, bent her head close and whispered, as for secrets:

"You're not going to school today. I'm gonna drown you! We're leaving Omaha!"

She tossed me, howling, into the car and started driving around, listening to me wail, waiting until I'd worn myself down and huddled myself into as small a ball as possible, shuddering with the knowledge that I was totally in her control.

Then she drove me to school. Stopped by the curb. Turned off the engine and sat for a long while, staring blindly through the windshield. Finally she turned and pushed open my door and, finally, looked *at* me. Pulled at the sleeve of my dress, straightening it out, then patted me on the arm absentmindedly.

"Have a good day, Doris. You look very pretty in your new dress. You see, I was right about the color. Perfect for you, isn't it?"

I stared at her through near-blindness born of fear. Her voice was perfectly calm and interested, her head cocked—I could almost see her planning our next extravagant shopping trip.

27

The morning's madness might never have happened at all. When I left her, she was smiling contentedly.

The course of my religious upbringing was total confusion. It had gained priority status in the endless battle Mom waged with Dad over everything. There was little Dad could say with which Mom would agree, but even so, trying to make me a Catholic when both she and Dad were Baptists was going to extremes.

I was flooded with doctrine at every Catholic service she made me attend. I was also, in this way, prevented from feeling any religious unity with my parents. I never had the slightest idea, in those early years, what I actually believed. No one seemed to notice the omission, and I certainly never mentioned it.

"She *is* a Catholic," I heard Mom yelling one night, after I'd gone up to bed. "It says so right on her papers, doesn't it?"

Papers? What papers? My ears stretched to the limit, and I held my breath, remembering that picture, so briefly seen, of the headless woman and myself.

"You have no right, Mac, to try to raise the child a different way than she was meant to be."

Dad ignored this.

"If it was moral obligation you were concerned with, Louise, I wouldn't be so opposed to this business. But you'd never have given a single thought to her being listed 'Catholic' on those papers if you hadn't gotten it into your head it would irritate me to death doing this!"

I couldn't hear her reply; it was low and venomous.

Dad's voice came then, quietly. "I wish you'd try to understand, Louise. I didn't choose this path. It was chosen for me."

But Mom said something else, and Dad made an exasperated, hopeless sound somewhere between a snort and a

28

grunt, and then Mom started yelling and I heard the front door slam and knew Dad had left her alone to her rage and gone for a long walk.

During this period I would dream about Josefine almost every night. I never *saw* her in my dreams. How could I, not knowing her? I dreamed a feeling I'd fabricated—it was all I had. An atmosphere warm with love and acceptance that made me that much sadder to wake and face true life.

After really bad days, I comforted myself with well-worn rationales. I assured myself that all kids occasionally wish they were adopted, when their parents make things tough. Believing your parents *aren't* your birth parents can give you a soothing remoteness. It means you don't have to care quite so badly about their meannesses and complexities.

And following along on this line of thought was the fiction that I was luckier than most, because I really *was* adopted. And since I didn't actually belong to Louise, it didn't have to break my heart that I couldn't make her love me. . . .

The summer I was thirteen, Mom took me to visit her family in Detroit. It didn't take a genius to suspect that the air force life, which meant my family life, was history. One more drop of emotional poison to add to oceans of insecurity.

My "real" mother had given me up. I was about to lose the only dad I'd ever known and loved. And while Josefine was a fantasy I could conjure at will, nothing else was. I was too young to know how to cope.

Detroit was another planet. Noisy, dirty, and thrilling. Street life that never seemed to quit, people out past the house laughing and shouting no matter what time it happened to be. Living with either Grandma—Mom's mother, whose house was in Highland Park—or with Aunt Ruth—

Mom's older sister, who lived right across the street from Grandma, officially in Detroit. The members of the family were so constantly in and out of each other's houses that I think most of the time there was no clear knowledge of who belonged where—everything was one big, continuous theater that housed the whole crew.

It was so totally different from the life I'd known that it wasn't even real; I was never in touch with the outer self other people believed was me. Instead, I stood back more and more, watching what went on, watching my own reactions in different situations and with different audiences. I felt the need for this act, as if I were in a play, onstage for my *life*. I'd lost whomever Doris McMillon had been, but according to the broad clues Mom continuously gave, there was nothing to mourn. *That* Doris rated poor as sin.

As for the other Doris, the Doris without a last name, the German Doris with a mother without a face and a father who'd never even entered the fantasy picture—well, that Doris might just as well never have existed. All the questions of her life remained, nagging, itching bits and pieces. But nothing followed on the heels of the questions except other questions, less and less endurable.

I was bitterly miserable.

It took two months of the summer of 1964 to learn I couldn't talk "proper" and be accepted on the street. It took my Dad one phone call after that to tell me I was deteriorating and to have a fight with Mom about it, long-distance. I made sure to use perfectly proper English when I spoke to Dad again. He was the only person who expected this double standard, but then he didn't share our new life in Detroit and so he didn't really understand.

In mid-July I got my period. I started wondering then what traits I might have inherited from Josefine. It had never occurred to me before, but it seemed suddenly important. Were there health problems she might have passed on? Were there private matters her daughter should know?

And what was she like in her character and personality? Had she felt the grown-up pride I was feeling when *she* became a woman? Had she wondered for years now about the mysteries surrounding boys? About liking them without understanding why she liked them and about wanting their approval?

Had *she* been immature in ways that embarrassed *me* in myself, or was she streetwise and cool and always on the edge of finding trouble for herself?

Mom took the opportunity of my new maturity to tell me some facts of life. She performed this necessary function leaning against the frame of the bathroom door, watching me as I sat on the toilet learning the ins and outs of sanitary napkins. I'd promised myself not to let her know when I started menstruating—everybody needs *some* privacy. But I should have known no one kept secrets successfully from Louise Evelyn.

"So . . ." She stared at me. "Now you can have babies."

I was silent. Having babies had nothing at all to do with my pride at having grown up.

"Blood always tells," she said cryptically, her favorite phrase, and whatever her own purpose in brandishing it, its effect was always exactly the same. It placed another woman, named Josefine, squarely dead center. It put fantasy ahead of reality, which was the only way I could be happy.

It occurred to me, not for the first time, that I didn't know what the word "privacy" really meant.

"They'll be all over you now," she decided, eyeing me as if she'd never seen me before that second. "Trying to get you on your back. Trying to get your little panties down, just like that woman. The free ride," she pronounced terribly, "has passed."

31

I didn't bother to pretend ignorance.

"Oral sex," she said suddenly, screwing up her lips and pointing her finger at my crotch as I stared at her, blank, still sitting on the toilet, the thrill of getting my period and feeling absurdly mature flaking to dread over what she was trying to impart.

"Never *ever* have oral sex. Fight them off, stop them, no matter what!" She was whispering. Secrets. "They'll all want to do it to you, so you remember, you do it even once, you're diseased and better off dead!"

Like Josefine? Was that one of the sins my "real" mother had committed?

I was starting to shiver, hugging the cold porcelain of the toilet seat with my thighs, and I discovered that evening, from the very first, the nervous nature of menstrual cramps.

Nobody asked me to have oral sex. Nobody asked me to have sex at all. Considering the buildup provided by Mom, it was a huge disappointment.

Dad called in the middle of August to ask Mom, once more, to come home. He'd been calling pretty constantly; she always agreed to talk to him, then the conversation quickly turned into a battle of accusations on her part and desperation, long-distance, from Omaha. Mom had made up her mind that Dad was seeing other women—that he'd cheated throughout their marriage. This wasn't exactly new; it had been her favorite tool to use against him for as long as I could recall.

She was always checking up on him when he was at work. Always cross-examining him when he was five minutes late getting home. She created an illusion of knowing *all!* It got so I was certain she could read minds and see through doors.

But her accusations that summer meant she'd already determined not to share the blame at all. If a divorce actually happened, and it looked as if it really might, it would be all Dad's fault. I was learning that about her. She made these decisions and set herself on a one-way course. Later she might regret it, but she never let herself change her mind back and never admitted she'd made a mistake.

And if Dad actually *became* a Baptist minister, well, she knew all about *that! She* knew how those damned women hung around the church lusting after men of the cloth!

The days pulled on to autumn and we didn't go home, and when Mom enrolled me in the Detroit public school system, I finally had to accept the fact that Omaha and Dad were gone.

I'd never been more than a mediocre student. We'd moved so often I'd never *finished* anything. Even so, I went straight to the head of my new class, which I felt said a lot about the Detroit public school system.

It made me wonder about education in Germany. About careers. Had Dad been right about the terrible problems I'd have faced, a black girl with a white mother like Josefine?

Out on Detroit's streets, I could have *been* in a foreign country—acceptance eluded me. The kids in the neighborhood thought I was an ass, partly due to Mom's attitude that I was "better" than they were, but also due to my truly incredible ignorance at times when I should have had some street smarts. A prime example was my famous phone talk with Dad during that summer vacation.

That two-minute chat was state-of-the-art. I'd never improve on it in all my life, though at the time I delivered my pronouncements with the innocence of social retardation, no malice intended.

"It's great here, Daddy." The words tumbled out all over themselves. After all, I had to stay interesting for him, and that meant saying as much in a short period of time as was possible.

33

"We go out all the time, to dinner and the movies and sometimes just for rides. . . . James, Mom's friend, has a 'deuce and a quarter.' . . ."

James was a steady companion of my mother's who took us around in his shiny new Electra 225. He was generous with his money, which was a treat for a kid who, dicounting her transient wardrobe, had always seen the pinched side of a penny. I didn't particularly like James as a person, but I dearly loved riding in his car, and besides, it was something to talk about to Dad.

"Put your mother back on, baby," he cut in after a bit. That was a first and should have warned me, but it didn't. Dad never went back to talk to Mom again; it was too much to expect from anybody.

I went and got her and took myself out to the front porch of my aunt's house. Some little time passed, and I had no inkling of approaching doom, enjoying myself talking to two of the kids from the neighborhood.

"Doris!"

Mom stood in the doorway, looking just past me, her foot tap-tapping. These were relatively new warning signals that something was wrong, that I'd made some terrible mistake, that I was in for it.

She glanced briefly at my face and wet her lips.

"Go take a bath."

I was startled. I never took my baths in the afternoon; there were so many people in and out, wanting the bathroom. As late at night as possible was the house rule, but there was Mom, tap-tapping with her foot, ordering me.

My box of Tide soap powder was over the sink. I measured it out with great care, disgusted that my hands were shaking. How could I be so scared over nothing? What kind of horrors could I possibly read into taking my bath early?

34

My morbid imaginings about Louise were becoming nearly as pervasive as my unrealistic fantasies of Josefine.

The bath water was foaming into the tub. I always let the tub get a couple of inches full, the bubbles silky and billowing, before I stepped into the middle of it all and let the water rise all around me and the heat rise up in waves over my head. I had my pants off and my shirt half-unbuttoned when, suddenly, the bathroom door smashed open, hitting me across the back and nearly throwing me face forward into the tub.

Mom stood there, hunched, her eyes funny.

"What are you doing, Doris?" Her voice was sharp, a nasty curl to it.

I gestured, frightened, toward the filling tub.

Her eyes shifted to the water, then back. They had that glaring look I hadn't seen in the three months we'd been in Detroit and that I'd convinced myself was part of her problems with Dad, not myself.

She advanced a step. "I told you to take your bath hours ago and you're still standing here, wasting time, wasting hot water. . . . I can't imagine how you'll ever learn to be responsible."

I'd been in the bathroom maybe five minutes, but I kept my mouth shut.

"Keeping everybody else waiting . . . Get in that tub!" her voice was rising.

I knew exactly what would happen. She'd start to bellow, full-steam, and then she'd start cursing. The fury would burst out through her fists—it was a lifelong set piece. It was the core of every atmosphere permeating the house. It was Louise.

I struggled with the remaining buttons on my shirt, and she closed the door and came closer in the tiny bathroom. I didn't mean to back away; I'd promised myself I'd never degrade myself like that again; I had to try to remember I was actually a woman; I'd gotten my period last month and everything!

Of course, none of that ended up counting. Not with the reality hulking in my face. The wall came up behind me and there was nowhere else to run and I stared at her, fascinated, as terrified as I'd always been.

Her features looked bloated.

"Get in the tub," she repeated, the words flattening together in a growl.

My shaking fingers wouldn't undo the buttons, and I still had on my socks. She made a move as if to push me flat out into the water, and I jumped to avoid the contact. She smiled, then, a secret little grimace, and looked around, eyes lighting on my bathtowel folded on the toilet tank.

She reached over and took the towel. Dropped it into the filling tub. I stared at the terrycloth soaking up all that water, flattening out all my bubbles, then she reached down and pulled the sopping towel up out of my bath and gripped the end and swung it, sudden, full-force, right at my head.

I think I screamed. It was terror. I didn't feel that first belt.

"Get in the tub," she roared at the top of her lungs.

I leaped to the right and landed, not past her as I'd hoped, but teetering against the rim of the tub. She darted at me and pushed hard, and I tumbled and landed down in the water, cracking my hip, hurting myself like hell. Then she was whipping at me with the soaking wet towel.

"Stop it!" The high, screaming voice didn't sound like me at all. "Don't hit me," I bawled. "I didn't do anything, just what you told me, stop it. . . . Stop it!"

Suddenly, the bathroom held someone else. I couldn't see past Mom, but I heard the grunting and cursing, and I thought, crazy thought, that somehow Dad had heard me

36

screaming from all the way back in Omaha and had come to rescue me.

It wasn't Dad. It was Aunt Ruth, taller than Mom by five inches, bigger by at least forty pounds, and if not nearly as mean, at least driven by expediency.

The water was still pouring into the tub around me. Rising, up to my breasts now, as I huddled down in the water, trying to disappear. It was hot, so hot, the bubbles rising, bizarre in their delicate fragility, and I saw a circus of arms and legs and heard muffled gasps and shouts and finally, out of it all, heard my Aunt Ruth's harsh voice.

"If you hit that child again, Louise, I'll beat the crap out of *you!* Stop thrashing around, Louise, and I'll think about letting go of you. Stop that vile screeching, good God, girl, are you totally demented . . . ?"

And Mom: "You bitch! Get away from me, you bitch! Nobody tells me what to do with my own child. I can do whatever I want with my own child! Get away from me. . . . I'll kill your ass, you bitch, who the hell do you think you are, I'll *kill* you! Do you hear me? I'll *kill* you!"

Then, suddenly, they were gone from the bathroom and the upstairs was silent. Totally, utterly still. Except for the roar and splash of the pouring water around my shivering body, making a temporary cocoon.

I was Louise's child, to do with as she pleased. Except when I was her *adopted* child, taken in at great sacrifice and reminded of it constantly. I was the child of a whore somewhere in Germany, who'd thrown me out, never having wanted me. I was Louise McMillon's replacement for her own daughter, Caroline.

I was all of these people, none of them having a steady

ego. What I *knew* was that I wasn't loved, and at that point in my life, nothing else had meaning.

I don't know why it seemed so certain that all my problems would be solved if I just found Josefine. I can't imagine why I thought I'd be happier in some way if I cleared up old mysteries.

I went to bed early that night and the next, emotionally worn out and utterly miserable, down to my last nerve and steeped in depression beyond my thirteen years. We'd gone back to Grandma's after the bathroom battle, so the escape to my bed had the protective effect of keeping me out of Mom's sight. There was no Aunt Ruth right downstairs now, to jump in and save my life. Grandma was too gentle to intervene. Too torn between confusion over the behavior of her own daughter and compassion for a grandchild she could do nothing to protect.

James came around before I went to bed, and Mom put on her welcoming company face. I was so grateful to James for just that simple fact, despite his loud laugh, gold tooth, peanut-shaped head, and cigar breath that he blew out between his lips while he talked.

That night they didn't go for a drive or to a movie. They sat in the living room, whispering and laughing. Grandma lived on the second level of a small, two-family house, which meant her rooms sat hip to hip without privacy, and since my tiny bedroom and the living room shared a common wall, it was hard to be totally deaf and withdrawn, no matter how much I tried to be. Even so, that night I fell quickly to sleep. I was exhausted, and besides, it was the best way to escape a situation that was threatening to smother me.

I dreamed. It was one of my fantasy dreams.

I sat at a table in a room whose walls I couldn't see. There was a plastic cloth on the table, a feeling it was yellow, a sense of sunlight in the room. I could smell the dream—it

38

was like coffee and sausages—and I was happy in the dream, knowing I wasn't alone at all, and that the chair across the table, pushed back a bit, was waiting for the woman humming, behind me, filling the dream with her presence.

Josefine.

I knew the dream would last only if I sat very still. It was vital not to turn my head to try to see. I knew that without having the slightest idea how I knew. Even when the thumping sound started, I didn't turn or let myself be tricked. It was only the kettle on the stove, steaming and bumping; it was only the rising shrill of the water boiling, nothing else; I wouldn't, I *couldn't* let myself try to see Josefine or I'd lose her completely. . . .

I woke from the soft dream, jerking to confusion, to a dark sense of impending disaster. The house was all whispers and hurrying footsteps, slamming drawers and doors, hissed commands—more a continuation of dreams than reality. All through, the banging and roaring was persistent, and after a while I realized the banging was somebody trying to bang in Grandma's front door and the roaring was somebody's enraged, vaguely familiar, shouting voice.

There should have been someone to answer the door. All that racket would wake the neighbors, and the man up the street just loved calling the police down on everybody. I thought about getting up and opening the door myself, then decided it was time to get smart and protect number one.

I shut my eyes as tight as I could, then a terrifying crash broadcast the front door flying open, followed by a bellow of pure outrage.

"Louise!"

I knew that tone—Dad at his rare worst, though how Dad could be in Detroit when he should have been home in Omaha. . . .

My God! It *was* Dad, breaking down doors!

The floor shook as he thundered into the living room. His shadow filled my doorway, the light behind him, his face completely hidden by the darkness in my room. Blinding light, then, and I curled tight, shielding my eyes, and he crossed the room and grabbed my shoulder and bellowed in my face.

"Where the hell is your mother, Doris?"

My mother had been right in the living room, only a few steps away, snug and immersed in James. And there was nothing clever I could think of to say because I finally understood that making Dad happy meant *not* answering this particular question.

"Where's your mother?" he asked me again, forcing his tone softer, letting go of my shoulder but clenching his fists.

"She was in the living room," I finally said, indignantly.

"And who the hell does this belong to?" he asked, trying to keep his voice reasonable, without much success.

I looked at what he was mashing in his hand. It was the straw hat James always wore on his peanut-shaped head.

I swallowed. "Uncle Bake?" I ventured, Uncle Bake being a legitimate member of the household and therefore not objectionable to anybody.

Dad's face sagged, though his shoulders and back, ramrod rigid, didn't relax or relent. He finished crumpling the hat into a totally unusable, unrecognizable ball.

"That's not your Uncle Bake's hat. His head's not that big," he said viciously, "and you *know* it, girl!

"Where's your mother?"

I'd managed a quick evaluation while Dad glared and mashed his fists. One of the sounds I'd heard minutes before was the sound of feet hustling out the kitchen door to the back steps.

But I only shook my head. The memory of yesterday's telephone talk with Dad, my mother's eruption into the

40

bathroom, the wet towel, my terror and revulsion, and the battle between Mom and Aunt Ruth that followed all made a vivid living picture, teaching me important late-learned lessons.

Dad wasn't hanging around for answers anyway. He'd figured it out for himself. He was gone, not out the back, thank God, but out the door he'd just come in.

I leaped out of bed and turned off the bedroom light, hurried back, huddled down, and pulled my cover over my head. Sooner or later, all the trouble would be mine; that was how these things worked out. Besides, this time I had to admit I wasn't innocent. If my sin was ignorance instead of malice, that couldn't be expected to count. If I'd kept my big mouth shut about James, Dad wouldn't have gone into a rage and wouldn't be in Detroit now, snorting for blood.

Long minutes passed. It felt like half the night. I was terribly confused, half-jerking with tension, wondering why my life was so melodramatic. Even if I hadn't been a confirmed dreamer, surely the real events that surrounded me were bizarre and unbelievable enough.

I kept thinking I heard sounds, but they were just house and street things, until Mom's voice came to me where I huddled under my covers. I couldn't make out who she was talking *to,* but I had the feeling it wasn't James and it wasn't Dad either; she sounded too hushed and subdued. Grandma maybe, or just muttering to herself.

Dad out the front door, Mom in the back. Round and round and round. I'd watched slapstick exactly like that on television, but the real-life version was something else.

Footsteps to my door again. Flash, and back on with my light. This time *Mom* stood over me, snatching away my blanket, grabbing a fistful of my hair, and shaking me by the head.

"Where's your father?" she hissed.

41

I mumbled something, flinching, and she glared into my face.

"Don't *act* like you were sleeping. I want to know what you told your father!" Shake shake shake.

"Daddy's in Omaha," I said stupidly, just before she yanked me off the bed.

Over to the bedroom window, then, dragging me by the hair. Her free hand balled into the back of my pajama top, and I heard the cloth rip. She peered through the glass, muttering to herself, then let go of my hair, keeping her grip on my shirt, and rammed up the window and dragged me half out, bobbing my head up and down with vicious little jerks.

"What—did—you—tell—your—father?"

Jerk jerk jerk.

I started to cry, picturing myself splattered on the asphalt, silly, dumb Doris, such an ass she actually fell out her bedroom window, leaving her poor, grieving mother, Louise, who'd taken her in when her own mother didn't want her, but then, her own mother was a whore, so that explained everything.

I only realized she was gone from the window and my bedroom too, when my head, too heavy for my mangled neck, fell suddenly forward, nearly pitching me over the sill. I caught myself, gasping, dragged myself back safe, and sank to the floor under the window, where I stayed.

The light was still on overhead. Harsh, colorless glare. My covers were swept off the bed, like me, dumped empty on the floor. The bedroom door stood open, all the way back to the wall. The living room, also lighted, beyond. was empty, no more footsteps, no more voices. Nothing from the outside stairs, front or back. The house might have been empty but for me, everyone in it dead and gone.

The silence inside my head was total.

That wasn't the end, of course. Dad called again, and the long-distance battles went on and on. But now there was definite talk of divorce. Autumn turned colors, and in spite of all my hopes, the day came when Mom and I went home. Not to be reconciled with Dad. Not to try again to make things work. To pack up the stuff we hadn't taken for our summer vacation and to leave Dad and Omaha for good.

I remember the Greyhound bus station. Dad standing watching the bus pull off. My sense of loss, held silent, all the pleading locked away, desperation choking me up. I loved him so dearly; he'd been the only consistently positive factor in my life, and I felt I'd never see him again or feel his warmth.

I was merchandise. Like my pretty, soon-gone clothes. Taken from one parent, given to two others, then removed from one of the two to be only Louise Evelyn's possession. To be put on show or punished—whichever mood she affected.

It had to have some root in my past. There had to be an inherited flaw that caused these terrible things to happen.

The bus pulled out. Dad was gone.

My dreams turned very bad after we permanently left Dad. Even fantasy failed; the dreams were dark, and once inside them I was trapped. I knew there had to be a door or window out or a switch for the lights, but I was too scared of what I might see to reach out and save myself.

I woke one night with my heart up in my throat. I'd felt a mocking presence beyond the darkness. Louise? Josefine?

Why did I feel that the presence was myself?

The furious phone calls continued between Dad and Mom, and Mom grew more and more venomous and uncontrolled. There were nights she'd suddenly erupt into my bedroom and start hitting me for no apparent cause. She'd always be screaming either about my own bad blood or about Dad's infidelity, and it was often Aunt Ruth who finally appeared to drag her off.

January. I was fourteen years old. We were staying with Aunt Ruth, and I'd spent a terrified half hour trying to dodge my mother and ending up being thrown around like a rag doll. That's when she started taunting me. Holding some papers in front of my face. Not close enough for me really to read and surely not close enough to snatch.

"You'd like these, wouldn't you, Doris? You'd love to see all the information on these papers. All about *you*, Doris. All the information about your adoption."

I reached out, shaking, and she slapped me across the face, holding the papers back just out of reach of my clutching fingers, over her head. I could hear myself making a terrible whining sound in my throat, and it scared me to sound like that; it terrified me that I could even smell myself—I was that frantic and off my head. Black print on white paper, whole lines lost in the marks of folds, but I saw one thing, leaping at me off the paper, capitalized. A name.

Josefine Reiser.

I must have fallen. I don't know. When I finally lifted my head, I was alone. I struggled to pull myself up off the floor. I had no clear thought in my head. I felt nothing, no pain, no fear, not even sadness or despair. I tugged off my pajamas and rummaged numbly in my drawer, taking the first sweater I found and the jeans I'd worn before. My boots were by the bed and I pulled them on as well. I was cold. I was amazed how cold I felt.

Reiser. Josefine Reiser. I knew her whole name; I could find her now. It was easy. Josefine Reiser. My real mother. The mother who loved me.

My coat was in the bedroom closet. My hat and gloves and scarf were there, too, and I wanted them all, yet left without them. My only focused thought was that everything would come right the minute I found Josefine.

I had no money; Mom made sure I was always short so that I had to go to her for things I needed, which meant I managed never to need much. That didn't seem to matter either. All that mattered was finding Josefine.

I crept downstairs.

The whole house was lit up, as if for a party. It was creepy, all that glare and no sound of anyone talking or moving. I was clutching my coat to my chest, and I stopped to try to get it on. Finally managed the sleeves, had trouble with the buttons, bent my head, found I couldn't see them properly, felt something cold and wet on my cheeks and chin, and realized I was crying dismally.

Absurd. I couldn't possibly go to Josefine crying.

That's when I realized I *needed* my hat and scarf and gloves. What was I thinking, being so irresponsible, going to my natural mother tear-soaked and frozen? But the thought of going back, all the way up all those steps, was too much for me. It seemed like a disaster; I was frozen to death; it was winter in the house and it was January everywhere else.

I stood staring blankly, numb with lethargy, aware of the needle-sharp need to get myself to safety, which meant leaving the lights and relative warmth of Aunt Ruth's house and putting a decent distance between myself and my mother.

There was the softest sound behind me, and I jerked around so fast I nearly lost my balance.

Mom stood in the kitchen doorway, eating ice cream from a chipped blue cup. Her spoon was in her hand; she was scooping it up and into her mouth, chewing—it was chocolate chip.

45

The last shreds of blind fantasy fled. *This* was the only reality.

"Where do you think you're going, Doris?" she asked, pushing in some more. Chew, swallow. Lick the spoon.

She was in her nightgown with her heavy black bathrobe on over it, the robe hanging open, the belt loose in the loops, and her pose relaxed and casual. Only her eyes glared, hot and small across the hallway.

She turned and put the cup down carefully on the table where Aunt Ruth left the mail for everybody. When she turned back to face me, she was pulling the cord out of her belt loops, winding it tight around both fists, then snapping it in and out between her hands and smiling at me.

Her voice was conversational. "I'm gonna *kill* you."

I hauled the front door open and raced down the steps and away down the street, the night air bitter on the tears still streaming down my cheeks, my back vulnerable if she chose to shoot me, throw a knife, bowl me down—there weren't many options she hadn't described to me in detail as I was growing up.

At the corner, I stopped. I turned and looked back. She was standing on the porch, shaking both arms in the air and yelling, "Come back here, I'll kill you! Come back here!"

I wondered, dully, if she was still brandishing the belt.

I turned again and ran around the corner, feeling safer out of her sight.

It was piercingly cold that night. I finally slowed to a walk, my breath frosting around my face, my skin stiff from the tears drying in their tracks.

My hands were balled to icy fists in my pockets, and I bent my head and kept walking. I hadn't watched the street signs, running blind, and now nothing looked familiar in the dark.

Some blunt facts pressed home. I was fourteen years old.

46

I was, at least for the time, totally alone on some street whose name I didn't know. At night, in Detroit. I had no idea how late it might be. I had no hat or gloves. I was freezing to death, and I had no money, which was worse.

I felt sick.

There was no one I could turn to. My father was far away. My Aunt Ruth, who'd helped me before, lived hip to hip with Mom, her own sister. Going to Aunt Ruth for help, which would mean returning home, seemed the height of imbecility.

And Josefine? Had I actually dreamed I'd find Josefine in Detroit, just because I needed something desperately and I'd always pinned her name to all my hopes?

Every effort I made to try to think fractured off into a frazzled, short-circuiting vagueness that had only one clear benefit: It protected me from any true understanding of how terrible my situation could conceivably get if luck deserted me entirely.

I'd nearly been thrown from a window. I'd nearly been strangled. My life was an endless list of such "nearlys" and I had no sense of normality to fall back on. In truthfulness, I had to consider myself lucky. "Nearly" had never been "actually." Such luck couldn't protect me indefinitely.

I don't know how long I walked on blindly, mostly in darkness, occasionally lit by an unbusted streetlight. I didn't see a single soul for all that time, but then, suddenly, up at the corner, the street was over-populated. Boys, a lot of them, smoking and laughing, horsing around, jabbing and punching at each other, then, God help me, noticing my arrival. I couldn't have conjured up anything worse, except maybe Louise, to horrify me.

A pair of them lounged down the street.

"Hey, darlin'." The taller of the two grinned, eyeballing me and cocking his head to the side. "Ain't she sweet?" he asked his friend, who was shorter and thicker and blowing smoke rings from a pouty little mouth in a head like a melon.

"Sweet," Melonhead agreed.

"Watchoo doin' out so late, darlin'?" asked Tall. "You lookin' for me?"

I couldn't think of anything less likely or more repulsive, but I forced myself to smile, stiff and sick.

"Hi," I said, my lips stuck to my teeth.

Tall looked at Melonhead, jabbed him in the chest, and they slapped each other's shoulders, howling in appreciation of how funny I was.

"She said 'Hi,'" Tall reported back to the group on the corner, which had fallen silent, watching.

"Where you off to, darlin'?" asked Tall, leering at me.

"My aunt's house," I said, surprised myself to hear it.

Tall eyed me, rubbed his hand over his chin, then glanced back over his shoulder, seeming to consider something. He shot a look at his buddy, said something, and shrugged, then grinned suddenly and bowed low to me, an exaggerated deep dip. Melonhead was already moving away, back toward the group, tugging himself tighter into his jacket.

There wasn't a sound from any of the other boys. They opened a path for me, though, and I forced my feet forward, staring straight ahead, up that narrow aisle, so close on either side I could feel the heat from their breath.

Then I was through. I didn't know why they'd let me off. I really wasn't stupid; I knew the kind of trouble I'd avoided. I also knew I couldn't break and run, that I had to just go on, cool and calm, and not look around. I imagined I could feel their concerted stare on my back. Then the light from their streetlamp was suddenly gone, not stretching as far as I'd finally walked, and the darkness closed in around me again and for the first time the darkness was on my side.

I took a deep, shuddering breath.

Going to my aunt? I'd said it without thought. But my

Dad's sister, Rosa Lee Smith, did live near here, if I was right about where I was. I could ask her to let me sleep over for the night. I could tell her what had happened, though I didn't for a minute think she'd believe my mom had threatened me; she'd think I was creating things to get attention for myself. Besides, I couldn't really imagine myself telling anyone that. I was ashamed. I saw all the fault as mine. Of course I was to blame, even if I didn't see how. Look at all the problems Mom and Dad always had. Look how they'd sacrificed everything to make me happy. Obviously, they'd sacrificed too much. Now we weren't even a family.

Feeling incredibly sorry for myself, I wanted only to get in off the street and sleep. I set off with more determination, up the block. I was fairly sure I'd been walking a straight line, that I was by now at least three miles from Grandma's, and that my aunt was two or three streets over, no more than a five-minute walk.

The street was perfectly empty again, and I was growing more and more aware of the miserable cold and especially of the numbness in my feet. My ears had reached a stage of burning pain, my nose was numb and running, and little gusts of wind kept getting caught up in my hair.

Trying not to concentrate on these matters, I suddenly realized I had company.

I must have been hearing it for some time, but my attention was diverted, turned inside myself, first thinking about how to get to my aunt's house quickly, and then trying to ignore how cold I felt. The sound was an echo of my own footsteps. Someone was following me on the cold cement.

I stopped. What I felt was mostly just tired to death. My thought was that they'd followed me after all, Melonhead and Tall and their buddies from the corner.

But when I turned, just wanting to get the worst over, only one man stood in the darkness, a few yards off.

He came a step closer, then stopped. I could barely see

49

him; I would have been totally blind but for the clearness of the night. It wasn't one of the boys from the corner. It was a man, older than the members of the gang, younger than my father.

I thought he smiled at me, but I couldn't really tell and I waited because there was nothing else I could do for myself.

"Hello," he finally said.

He had a chocolate kind of voice, soft and too smooth, but maybe I was just hypersensitive that night.

"Don't be afraid," he said. "Please. I won't hurt you."

"No," I said wearily. "I'm not," I added, not very coherent.

"My name's Tom," he said, "and I'm a social worker. I work that group you passed a couple of blocks back. That's why they let you pass. Because they couldn't afford any little amusements just then."

I didn't know if he wanted my thanks. I remained silent.

"I thought it might be just as well to give you an unofficial escort," he said calmly. "After all, it is late and you are very young and you didn't mention how far you were going, did you?"

I held to my dogged silence, too tired to formulate answers.

"I think you said you were going to your aunt's house?" he asked, unperturbed, patient, just as dogged.

"My aunt's house," I repeated, stupid with deepening exhaustion. The night would never end. I'd never in life find sanctuary.

He studied me for a long minute, then placed his hands with care into his jacket pockets.

"You're out very late for such a young girl. And you were very lucky that was the only gang you met, and that they weren't without guidance tonight. Do your parents know you're out to visit your aunt at one in the morning, all by yourself?"

It was none of his business what my parents knew, but then he was a social worker, or so he said, and I guess he was used to asking any questions he chose. Besides, if he was really what he claimed, and I couldn't see any reason for him to lie about it, then I really was grateful he'd been there, on that street corner.

"Oh, my parents know," I made a great effort, improvising brightly, "My mom's sick and my dad's out. And Mom sent me to my aunt's for some medicine."

He absorbed this in silence, then moved a step closer, and I moved a step back. He held up his hand in a placating sort of gesture, palm toward me, and shook his head.

"You're running away from home, aren't you?" he asked abruptly.

I didn't own much cool and I lost what I had, staring blankly at him, wondering how the hell he knew.

"I'm going to my aunt's," I repeated flatly.

He ignored this. "Do you have somebody you can talk to?" he asked gently. "This 'aunt'?"

"I can talk to my aunt," I said, taking another step backward. "I can talk to my minister, too," I added, feeling this to be a true inspiration. "If I had anything I needed to talk about I'd find somebody to talk *to*, but I don't." I made it another step backward, then another, but he didn't move. "And I really do have to get that medicine for my mother, she could die. . . ." But I sensed that was pushing it too hard. "I'm sorry, I shouldn't be wasting all this time, hanging around, talking, thanks about back there, on the corner, with those boys. . . ."

And then I turned and ran, flat-out, half-falling down the street, terrified to look back, and suddenly there was my aunt's house up on my right. I had no breath left, and no imagination either. All the devils of my childhood had already popped out of the woodwork to terrify me.

I stumbled onto my aunt's porch and pounded unrestrained on the door, and after a long wait it was my cousin, Linda Gail, who opened up a crack, on the chain, to look out.

My aunt was not at home. My mother had called in hysterics, and Aunt Rosa Lee had gone out on the street to search. She wasn't the only one apparently. Mom had phoned all the other relatives and friends and acquaintances in easy reach and, finally, the police.

Linda Gail let me hide in the basement, then ruined the gesture entirely by blurting out my presence there the minute her mother came in.

"This is wrong, baby," my aunt stared at me, but there was compassion in her eyes that convinced me she knew well enough my mother was a little off. "Your mother's worried to death, crying to break her heart. I'm gonna call her and tell her you're here, and safe, and that I'll bring you home in the morning after breakfast."

I knew nothing I said would change her mind so I didn't bother to try. After all, what did I expect? My mother was—my mother.

That was Saturday night into Sunday. I arrived back home Sunday noon. I hadn't eaten anything at my aunt's; I felt desperate and sick. I didn't know what Mom would do.

But she didn't do anything at all. Not right then, with my aunt standing in the door. She didn't look at me, and her foot tap-tap-tapped while she thanked my aunt for bringing me home and suggested I go to my room to consider the pain and fear I'd caused everybody who loved me.

I stayed in my room, in terror, throughout that day, waiting for her to decide I'd stewed long enough, waiting for whatever horror she'd dream up. That something would happen I never doubted for an instant.

I spent the time dreaming about Josefine. If I closed my eyes lightly, I could conjure an image. It had never upset me, this thought of a heritage mixed not only by race but also by nationality. It was romantic, a mystery, and it meant I could draw Josefine to any form and color that pleased me. That night I made her tall and slim and beautiful and, of course, blond. Germans were, weren't they? It was my favorite image—I imagined her with the frailty of vulnerability. This little touch placed Josefine a universe apart from Louise.

Of course, Josefine never got older. Never, from the postwar years when she'd had to give me away until the moment of my latest fantasy. To have aged her might have made her real. What I needed then wasn't reality.

She was gentle and gracious and wise. Oh—and she loved me.

She had to love me. I was *her* child. As someone named Caroline was Louise's real child. You had to love your own child.

I'd determined that nothing Louise said about Josefine could ever be allowed to count. Josefine wasn't evil, dirty, or diseased. She certainly wasn't a prostitute. She'd been little more than a child herself when she'd had me. She was white and my father black. I was the product of a star-crossed love affair—how romantic. And however it had happened, Josefine was brokenhearted when she knew she had to offer me for adoption.

On this meager diet, I lived through that endless day.

That night, before I went to sleep, Mom finally came to my room. I'd been waiting and waiting, wondering which personality would come through the door. When she finally appeared, she stood in the doorway forever, then went to the window and stood looking out, silent for so long I grew more and more fearful.

I'd been huddled under the covers, but I pulled myself up cross-legged, on top of the spread. When she spoke, it was

53

without turning. Her voice was exhausted and without in-flection. It was the other Louise. Generous, overworked, misunderstood Mom.

"Tomorrow, after school, don't dawdle coming out. Your aunt and I, we'll be there to pick you up. The police want to talk to you."

She did turn then.

"I reported you missing, of course," she said angrily. "After all, I couldn't very well let a young girl like you wander around on your own in Detroit. It was a wicked, thoughtless thing to do, Doris. I'm pained and disappointed in you; there are no words to describe the grief you've caused, or how sick you've made me."

I stared at her, fascinated. Not for the first time, I felt my mind bending, threatening to bow to this assessment of my-self. Except that this time, I found I was very, very angry, an anger I wisely kept silent.

"Then, when your aunt was good enough to call, when I could finally calm myself and realize you weren't lying dead and raped in an alley somewhere, I called the police back and told them you'd been found.

"Anyway"—she finally looked directly at me, and I felt a different kind of fear. She seemed so strange, so jumpy with the weariness—"they want to see you. I think they may want to lock you up." She rubbed dully at her mouth. "I may let them. Certainly nothing I've tried has worked. You're a bad girl, Doris. It's in your blood."

She took her hand from her lips, and I saw the fingers tremble in that second before she pushed both hands into her pockets and turned to leave my room.

"I'll decide what to let them do with you tomorrow."

FOUR

I NEVER DOUBTED THE decision would be up to Mom. Didn't she rule my life completely? I was always so frightened of what she'd do, even when I'd been most careful to be good. My own actions didn't seem related at all to her *reactions*.

I realize now that Mom wasn't just reacting in a vacuum. She must have been deeply hurt by my nagging, endless questions about my birth and adoption and my "real" mother. It must have been the sort of anguish that grows to a bitter, chronic pain; she did know I was a dreamer, and she must have guessed the focus of those fantasy hours.

I don't think she was capable of coolly reasoning it all out. She wouldn't see she'd initiated my preoccupation with Josefine by the very attempts she made, continuously, to protect herself. All she'd know was that her worst fears had actually come true.

Her little girl, her pretty, dressed-up doll, wasn't the perfect daughter, adoring and lovable, wasn't *hers*, body and soul, but instead was merely a frightened, discontented child.

I don't know if she had any idea of the mental anguish she was causing. I believe the majority of her words and actions were helpless short circuits, with her need to protect herself her supreme consideration, preventing any empathy. Of course, I need to believe that. It's my only consolation. And certainly knowing what I know now about her lifelong emotional problems, it's easier to believe that she couldn't possibly have understood the devastation she was causing.

But these understandings came slowly, with maturity and a family of my own. Back then, I merely functioned minute to minute, trying to survive a child's confusion. I was fourteen years old, and what was real for me then was all the horrors I could create, about Mom, about myself, about the coming appointment at the police station.

I spent the night unable to sleep, unable to relax at all. The bed got hot, the sheets tangled with my tossing. I kept thinking that Mom could tell any tale she chose, for whatever her purpose. I could even be put in jail for the rest of my life if that's what she decided she wanted.

I remember all this clearly. Bad memories are supposed to fade with time, but this one defied the passing years and softer considerations too and stayed vile for me. The very texture of my blanket, balled and clutched to my hot face. The bitter bite of the air when I stood, trembling, at the schoolyard gate, spotting Aunt Rosa Lee's car waiting. The surge of sudden nausea that was so intense it would have been disastrous if I'd been able to eat anything since the day I'd run away.

I remember all the thoughts knocking around in my head on the drive to the police station. I remember wondering if they needed evidence to uphold whatever your mother said about you. I wondered if anybody but me really *did* know Mom was nuts, because she was nuts, wasn't she? Even if I was somehow the cause, she really wasn't normal. It couldn't be normal to act that way toward a daughter.

Of course, if she knew the extent of my fantasies, wouldn't that make her wild? Wouldn't that even justify her rage, her calling the police, her branding me a runaway? These new guilty thoughts chased around in my head until I blessedly couldn't think at all.

It was a terrible night, a horror-filled day, an interminable ride to the station. Aunt Rosa Lee, Aunt Ruth, Mom, and Grandma were all there, but nobody was saying anything. From the second I got into the car at Durfee Junior High, no distractions saved me from the nightmare of my thoughts.

Finally, we arrived. My impression, terrified as I was, was of a stark building, gray and threatening. Halls too wide. Doors too high. Light filtered hard and colorless through dirty windows. Aunt Ruth was grim and silent, her eyes sliding uneasily from side to side. Grandma just stomped along, bringing up the rear, staring at everything with dreary concern. Mom was rigid, silent, and righteous, her black umbrella clutched like a club in her hand.

The room for our meeting had a long, battered table with chairs pulled up on both sides. The one at the head of the table had the only high back, and its seat was discolored by a big pink stain that looked sticky and damp. No pictures brightened the walls, although something in a frame—a certificate or something similar, not meant for decoration—was nailed to the wall between the two high windows. The deep shadows in the room engulfed the print and made it unreadable.

Venetian blinds made slatted shadows over everything.

There were radiators. They kept clicking and spitting. The room wasn't very big, so it seemed too full of people. There was a policewoman in uniform plus a man who did most of the talking—I never was sure if he was a police officer or a social worker. Then, another man, and a woman over at a small table by the side wall.

My Mom. Aunt Ruth. Aunt Rosa Lee. Grandma.

I got to sit in the chair with the stain, and everybody stared and shook their heads at whomever was asked each question. Maybe they were memorizing everything said to check up on it later. I kept shivering and yawning, filled with yet another horrible thought. What if they asked if I was "real" or adopted? Would that affect whatever they did to me, or didn't it matter?

"I understand this isn't the first time your daughter has run away from home."

Mom didn't comment. Neither did anyone else.

"Is that true, Doris?"

"I never ran away," I said, terrified.

Everybody stared at me politely.

"I go for walks," I added hopefully.

"Why do you feel the need to go for these walks?"

I'd already determined to stick as much to the truth as possible, to avoid getting tangled up later.

"My mother spanks me a lot," I muttered through my teeth, not daring to look at her, "and I'm tired of it, so I go for long walks."

The room seemed to swell then with noise, Mom's roar dominating everything. I shut her out, not wanting to hear again about my sinful ungratefulness, or what a disappointment I was after the sacrifices Mom had had to make all my life. I even closed my eyes, willing myself away, and when Mom started shouting at the top of her lungs, I jerked up and out of my chair, sure as anything that she was screaming at *me*.

I'd made it all the way to the door, stopped there by the policewoman and unaware, in my flight, that everyone else in the room was dividing their astonished attention between my raving mother and my terrified self.

58

Aunt Ruth told me later that they'd asked Mom where my dad was.

I put my hands over my ears and huddled against the door, the policewoman hovering near me, and it seemed they were all moving, all the shadows in that place, shifting without purpose, making me feel sick and cold all over again. And my mother was screaming, swinging her black umbrella, swinging it violently at whomever she might hit—the social worker, Grandma, the policewoman. . . . I didn't understand a single word she howled; she'd reached that incoherent level of absolute rage.

Suddenly, I was being bundled out of the room, and the policewoman's body screened out the view. I heard the words "protective custody" through a numb confusion. Outer office. Gray corridor. I was pulled and hustled so fast I couldn't feel the linoleum under my feet. Out onto the lot and over to a parked squad car. And suddenly, horribly, there was Mom, running toward us, screaming curses and whipping her umbrella at the air.

I threw my arms up over my head as I was tossed into the back seat of the squad car, then the door slammed shut and Mom erupted all over the place.

"You can't take my child away," she was screaming. "That's *my* child, you can't take her away from me, you can't tell me what to do with my own child, I'll kill you, I'll kill all of you . . . !"

She scrambled onto the hood of the car, slamming on the windshield with her umbrella gripped in both fists, the tears streaming down her cheeks.

It didn't prove anything, of course. I was gone.

Another ride, this time with strangers, police officers. A building without a label as my final destination. And those words—"protective custody"—providing no comfort.

Looking back, I'm impressed by how quietly I sat, but in

59

truth, I think the silent immobility was shock, not cool—I'd gone inside myself. I remember staring out the front window, past the driver's head, then sneaking a glance at the policewoman beside me in the back seat, and finally, looking swiftly away.

She was staring out her own side window, and her face was grim. At the time, I thought she was angry with me. Now I understand she was painfully tired of the whole thing. She wasn't young, and it was safe to assume she'd been at this for years. Dealing with a social structure she'd come to disdain.

It must have been exhausting, year after year. Watching the same scenarios unfold in that depressing room—abused children who became runaways, from broken homes. It must have been essential to stay remote and uninvolved. There wasn't any other way to do the job.

I didn't understand that then. I was only a child. I understand it now only because my own work makes personal involvement emotionally devastating if I allow it.

And even today, trying to be objective, I can't conceive of that stay in "protective custody" ever having happened if I'd been white or my family had been in different circumstances. But for a black child then, in Detroit, it was the easiest and fastest solution.

"Belt."

I watched it join the small pile of my belongings.

"Shoelaces."

I didn't have any, which seemed to irritate the matron.

"Watch."

Maybe they thought I could manage to choke myself on the tiny strap. They even confiscated the elastic belt for my sanitary napkins, substituting tiny pins instead.

Protective custody.

It couldn't possibly still be Monday afternoon, but it was. Still bitter outside, like Saturday night, and not over-warm

60

inside juvenile hall. Next stop was a long narrow room full of shower heads. The tile was discolored; the room smelled from damp, decay, and other unsubtle things.

A girl already stood in the showers when I arrived. She was naked and wet and singing at the top of her lungs.

"Hey, girl." She flipped her head, rubbing her palms over her hips. "I'm Peaches, pleased to meetcha, we'll be doin' the new kid number together. . . ."

She soaped her small breasts with a vigor that was miraculous considering the freezing cold in the shower room and the tiny chip of soap and the need to use your hands like a washcloth since there was nothing else.

"B 'n' E for me. Whatchoo here for, honey?"

I couldn't come up with anything worthy of winning points, but Peaches accepted my silence as normal, nodding her head and wiggling under the water.

The shower was frigid. The floor around the drain was crusty under my feet. There were little paper hand towels for drying off, the kind you get in ladies' rooms in restaurants. Brown and thin and sharp on soft spots. The police-issue T-shirt the matron provided was discolored and stiff, topped by a hideous shift that had a tear in the hem and that didn't fit. It was damn lucky I didn't believe any of it.

It was late, well past dinnertime, when the matron walked us up, stopping at each of a series of doors to unlock, then relock. Upstairs, then, on wide shallow steps, and the walls were colorless—gray or tan, I never knew which, the light was so bad.

It was the most terrifying walk of my life. I didn't understand what I was doing there, with Peaches, in for B 'n' E— I also had no idea what *that* meant.

Our final destination was a room full of girls. The lighting was overhead bulbs, long and filthy so that all the colors contained there were dull—the walls, floor, depressing tables and chairs, even the shifts and T-shirts we wore. All the tables seemed just a little too low. The chairs too narrow. There was an old, very small black-and-white TV on a ledge, heavily chained to the wall.

There was one tattered, threadbare rug in the middle of the room. Each of the girls seemed to go out of her way to avoid it.

A redhead, Small Sally, hunkered over the television. She informed Peaches and me that she was in charge of turning it off and on and tuning it. Apparently, there was somebody in charge of everything. The stand-out was Tommie T, who was big and vicious around the mouth and pregnant as all hell on size ten flat feet. Tommie T was blankets and sheets.

A tray arrived with two cups of milk and a plate of graham crackers. Supper for me and Peaches—dinner was history. Peaches pulled me aside under a silent, group stare, and divided up the cookies quick—one two three. They were stale, but I was hungry, in spite of being scared shitless. It surprised me to see the milk wasn't full of disgusting wax chunks, but I decided to leave it anyway and not press my luck.

That's when I first realized I had nothing from home. Not a nightgown or pajamas. Not a clean change of underwear for tomorrow. Not even my toothbrush.

Small Sally looked astonished when I mentioned it.

"Toothbrush?" She looked me up and down, maybe trying to decide whether I was actually serious. "You don't get nothin' like that right off, you gotta be here a while before they go give you toothbrushes and things. Just where the hell you think this *is*, sis?"

I found a small, round table shoved over in the corner, pulled up a tiny chair a second-grade kid might have fit into, and huddled there, miserable, trying not to look crunched, while Peaches pushed her way cool and brassy into a prominent place by the comic books. After that, time stopped passing while my heart bumped around and I waited to be challenged. I was *sure* I'd be challenged.

When lights out finally came, I was so tired I'd nearly

62

stopped being afraid. I was numb and half-asleep in my chair. The matron came to lock us into our individual cubicles. The place was so overcrowded that some of the girls, rotating around, were always sleeping in the main room on cots instead of safe and secure in the sick-smelling little cells.

I was taken to a cubicle. After all, I was new. There was a pane of glass on the door, the glass barred over and covered with mesh. There was a toilet in the corner. It was rusted and brown. There was a sink as well, and the whole room stank from old urine.

The only positive thing to be said was that the closing of the door finally shielded me from the glazed glare of Tommie T, the blanket and sheet girl. She'd made me her focus for all that time, until the other girls finally noticed and giggled and whispered, avoiding me totally, and Tommie T as well.

The challenge hadn't materialized at the end of that first night, but I knew that it would if I had to stay in "protective custody" long enough.

No matter which way I looked at it, I couldn't convince myself there was anything normal about my life. I was too emotionally drained at the time to wonder if it was just bad luck hounding me around, or some taint I'd inherited at birth. After all, how many kids at age fourteen have incited their mothers to actual violence, over and above the half-serious threats you hear in any household?

I don't know how much it would have mattered to me— knowing I was adopted. I think I would have wanted to learn all I could, anyway, about my natural parents. I can't stand secrets, and I'm naturally curious. But I never had the chance to let my curiosity develop naturally. From that day I was five and about to be naturalized, I knew, from Mom's attitude, that there was something very wrong, and the years that followed, for whatever the cause, were disastrous.

I watched the shattering of the only family I knew, and in that flying debris I lost Dad, who loved me. I lost a whole way of life when Mom took me to Detroit, which meant I no longer even minimally fit in anywhere. I was the brunt then of all my mom's pain and rage, and it didn't matter at all that she was clearly sick. I didn't know what caused the emotional illness, so I naturally assumed the cause was me.

But the very worst thing to happen in my life was that stay in "protective custody." It demeaned me in a way I'd never forget.

Could growing up black with my "real" mother in Germany really have been worse than this?

For most terrible by far, looking back on those days and the anguish they caused, was the constant, bitter question I kept asking myself.

Why? That one word encompassed all the other questions.

Why did Josefine give me away? Was it because I was black, and so she didn't want me?

Why did Louise want me dead? And if she didn't mean it, why did she say it? Was it because I was half-white, and so she couldn't love me?

Why was I here, locked up with these girls? This was jail, wasn't it, for people too young to go to a regular prison? So what was I doing here? What was my crime?

Even now, grown up and faced with the ugly realities thrown at me by my job, I can't truly begin to comprehend anyone doing that to a young girl. It wasn't just the physical fear and revulsion, though they were bad enough. It was the mental and emotional confusion of not knowing what I'd done to deserve such punishment.

No one told me. No one said it would come right. No one talked to me about any of it at all.

And whatever Louise's purpose in labeling me a runaway,

it could easily have backfired. I could have been made a ward of the court and placed with a foster family. I could have been taken away from Louise, which seemed to be her greatest fear—these things happened daily. Not that I *knew* that then; I only feared it.

And I was quite sure that if I hadn't actually done anything wrong, anything criminal, then this latest punishment must be because I was adopted. It was the only thing separating me from "normal" people.

The Tuesday I spent in protective custody was the longest day of my life. I was surprised to have slept deeply, dead to the world; it was misery when they got me up. I had to join the other girls, and it was a replay of Monday night. Nothing to do after getting down the sticky lumps they called oatmeal and the ever-present cup of milk.

I'd read all the comic books by ten o'clock. There didn't seem to be anything worth watching on TV, and besides, I found out quickly enough that you were expected to slip Small Sally an incentive if you wanted her to try the stations for you since she wouldn't let you try them yourself.

And nobody left for school. School, I was told, was one of those privileges like a toothbrush. You aspired to it only when you'd been here long enough.

A small, thin girl named Katie sat with me at the smallest table. She had heavy circles under her eyes, which made her look older than I did, but she grinned a lot, without upsetting the circles at all, and was open when I timidly asked her why she was here with this bunch of oddballs.

She shrugged. "Oh, I stabbed my stepfather in the face," she said, eyeing me.

"Stepfather," I said, blankly.

"Well, actually, not exactly," she admitted as if I'd seriously questioned the term. "Not like being married to Mama, not like that, but *there,* don't you see, which is the same thing, isn't it?"

She seemed suddenly concerned about the truth of this point, and I hastened to reassure her, wagging my head up and down hard.

"I mean, it's important when it's family, they make it a whole other thing. . . ." She had her lip between her teeth and was chewing it, worried. "I wouldn't like to think they'd go pull that shit on me now. . . ." Her face screwed up for tears. "After all, what the hell difference did it make whether he married her or not?"

"No difference," I fell over myself to assure her.

She looked vastly relieved and pushed back her hair. "Wish I'd aimed better," she leaned close to confide, "and killed the bastard. Now all I get's more of the same if I ever get out of here at all."

I took myself off to a separate little table and started giving some serious thought to survival. I focused on immediate need—comforts and necessities the other girls seemed to have that I was lacking and that I could remedy. For a start, there were no sheets on my bed. No blanket. No pillow—certainly not. I'd been too exhausted and depressed the night before to care. Now I felt different. I was starting to get mad.

After all, what the hell was I doing here with this bunch of horrors? It was Mom who was nuts, and me who was locked up. My fear faded behind growing outrage.

It became more and more important as the morning inched away to stop being a victim and try to make myself more comfortable. I knew where the closet with the sheets and blankets was. Nobody was watching me. I went to set myself up.

The room was small, shelved on three walls, the shelves piled with sheets and uniformly thin, dun-colored blankets. I selected a sheet that didn't look too yellow and a blanket that didn't smell too moldly and was turning to go and make up my bed when, suddenly, the little room darkened as the light was blocked from the corridor.

66

It was Tommie T, of course. The pregnant sheet and blanket girl.

Tommie T advanced a step, which brought her right into my face, and snarled. Actually did that, pulled back her lips, lowered her head as if she meant to butt, and snarled.

"You don't *bring* your ass in here, fool! This is *my* room. If you ever get sheets, and it ain't highly likely, if you ever do get sheets, it'll be because *I* give them to you! You stupid little ass-lickin' shit. You ever come in here again, I'll *kill* you!"

It was a really poor choice of threats. After all, I'd heard those words since I was a small girl, and that from a *real* badass. I'd never considered standing up to Louise Evelyn, but Tommie T was just a fat, nasty bitch and nothing to me.

One day in the slammer. I went apeshit.

"Now *you* listen, bitch!" I heard hissing between my teeth, driven past my limit. "You think you're about to fuck with me, think again! You're gonna have that baby a whole lot sooner than you know if you don't get out of my face!"

She backstepped, head tilted, hands on her hips. There was no surprise on her face—there wasn't anything. I'd been so quiet and so withdrawn, I'd been too easy to read. And suddenly I wasn't easy, but that didn't mean I'd won, just that she'd wait and see. For the moment, she watched me with that narrow, blank stare, then she let me take my blanket and sheet and leave.

Lessons. Never tell your father your mother has men friends. Never be so meek and quiet you're labeled a helpless little shit.

At one-fifteen, a mystery lunch was served. My most engrossing task for the day became figuring out exactly what it was. I finally decided that the soup was split pea, so thick it formed knots in my throat, and that the red stuff they had in a bowl by the bread wasn't jelly at all, but cherry Jell-O, and that I was expected, like the other girls, to spread it on the stale bread.

It took an eternity, but Tuesday finally ended as everything finally does. Katie told me that Wednesday was the regular day for the corrections people to decide who stayed and who went home. All the girls got lined up on Wednesdays at nine o'clock sharp. If somebody came to bail you out and to promise to take responsibility, you could go home—or possibly not—the specific ins and outs of this process were as shrouded in mystery as Tuesday's lunch.

There were twenty of us, studies in absolute and morbid silence. No laughing or joking or arguing or posing. Back down through the doors Peaches and I had entered Monday night, with the stop to unlock, go through, stop, relock. Back, finally, to the first floor and the counselors' offices.

It was agony. I didn't know if Mom had come—nobody told me. I couldn't imagine actually wanting her there, but staying at juvenile hall wasn't much of an alternative.

And the other horrors I'd imagined about the ease of being "put away" because I was only adopted—well, that was a nightmare for me. I was absolutely sure no foster home or orphans' home or any other new unknown would be for my benefit.

But of course Mom came, with Aunt Ruth. I should have had more faith. Mom wasn't one to leave the decisions to anybody else. Our little meeting with the counselor took two minutes flat. Mom had to promise she'd take care of me so I could leave protective custody. She solemnly vowed to see I didn't run away again, and Aunt Ruth agreed to share in this awesome responsibility.

Mom and Dad were formally divorced later that same year.

FIVE

I WALKED ON EGGSHELLS from that point forward, trying to do whatever my mother seemed to want, but never able accurately to gauge and so never really accomplishing it. I found myself living a more and more pervasive fantasy life—sinking into frequent depressions, no doors or windows out of this trap. Envisioning romantic conversations and situations centered around a woman I'd never even met. And all the while I was wondering what I'd inherited from those faraway strangers—my biological mother and dad.

A month after juvenile hall, I had a meeting with my two favorite teachers, Elaine Hoover and Abe Ulmer. My home situation was no secret to Mr. Ulmer. He'd acted as friend and adviser over and over when I'd come to school still smarting from the latest battle with my mother. I'd made it a habit to shelter in the dim silence of the library, and Mr. Ulmer always ran me to ground, then listened without lecturing to the confusion and anger I could no longer keep totally private.

One day, I told Mr. Ulmer about being adopted. I never had before; it was my shame, my deadly little secret. It meant that I was unforgiveably different, and I hated that so much—being different. I was too young then, and too personally involved, to realize all kids that age strive to be like their peers.

But I opened up to Mr. Ulmer. And once I'd actually said it, told him I was adopted, I felt the oddest sense of peace, of separating myself from my chaotic home life.

It was a totally new realization, and it stunned me. I couldn't know what I'd inherited from my natural parents, it was true, but I *did* have this assurance. No way would I personally reflect Louise McMillon's madness. She wasn't my "real" mother.

Once I started talking to Mr. Ulmer, I couldn't stop. It was such a new and cathartic release for me. I knew he genuinely cared about my welfare. He was a good and gentle man, and hated all injustice. But I was wrong in considering his interest merely passive. He was the person who presented me with real life prospects.

He and Elaine Hoover told me about a scholarship program funded by the John D. Rockefeller Foundation. It was called "ABC"—"A Better Chance"—and if I could pass the secondary school admissions test with high enough scores, I could escape from Detroit, my mother, and my growing sense of hopelessness.

That afternoon, I went home to Grandma's in a haze that shut out thought. I got undressed, though it was only four o'clock, and into my pajamas and under the covers, my arms and legs trembling, a quaking in my chest and my fingertips and toes like ice. Bits and pieces of my conference with my teachers kept drifting in and out of consciousness.

I was unbearably excited.

This was news that needed sharing, or else I'd burst. Yet the impulse was strong not to share it with my mother. Her reactions were never what I wanted. Instead I lay there,

70

imagining telling Josefine my news. I knew exactly how she'd look. The quick pride on her face would give me a sense of worth. Her whole attitude would tell me that her love for me was more important to her than her own needs, and that she'd always want the best for me—she always had. Wasn't there proof enough? Hadn't she ignored her own feelings when she'd given me up for adoption and a vastly better way of life in America?

Unfortunately, I was too excited to be content with a make-believe conversation inside my own head. The real conversation was waiting to happen in Grandma's kitchen, with Louise, not Josefine.

I climbed back out of bed and put on my jeans and a soft old shirt, then went in to dinner, sucked air, and told Mom, Aunt Ruth, and Grandma about the scholarship and the test and the possibilities.

"You'll take the test." Mom slammed the table with her fist. "You'll score higher than anybody else!" Her face was growing belligerent, as if anyone was disputing it.

"You'll go to that private school because this is your big chance, and you'll be at the top of your class!"

Then she sat there glaring and nodding her head and muttering under her breath.

Well, I'd been really excited and without any doubts. I was afraid, of course—I wasn't a total ass. I was afraid because this was so important to my life. This opportunity was a once-in-a-lifetime chance—I was hyped-up deaf and blind and numb. That is, until I understood that Mom desired this thing that *I* wanted, at which point I became equally sure that if Mom was so hot on my trying for this plum, there had to be something rotten about it.

But there really wasn't any question about taking the test. Winning the scholarship meant going away to a select Massachusetts boarding school and learning about real life. I'd meet new people—a different class of people. . . .

That thought burned. It seem disloyal, an admission I

71

was not content, not proud enough of what I already had. But I really couldn't stifle the obvious facts. Detroit, for me, at that point, was a desolate dead end. The ABC Program meant limitless chances to find out who and what I could be.

Besides, if I didn't take the test, or if I took the test and didn't pass, or if I passed but didn't score high enough to win the chance, Mom would kill me. There was always that added incentive if I needed it.

I took a tiny Bible along with me the day of the test. We'd been told not to bring *anything,* but I snuck it into my desk. I viewed it as extra, legitimate help. I didn't let myself even consider doing less than my absolute best. Windows close. Doors open. Opportunity strikes if you're ready, and I was ready. I wasn't about to be robbed of my chance.

My scores came back high. I'd amazed even myself. And a few weeks later I was accepted by one of the best schools in the country—Concord Academy.

"What kind of orientation?" Mom's foot was back to its tap-tapping.

I looked at her, helpless, not sure how to explain so she wouldn't either accuse me of talking down to her or start yelling that I was being secretive.

Josefine, I thought angrily, would have sat down and talked it all out with me intelligently.

"It's like a preview for what school will be like in the fall." I made my tone comforting. "They make sure all the new students are prepared, you know. They want everybody to feel comfortable. Fit in . . ."

That was a mistake.

"Fit in?" Her eyes widened, then narrowed, considering. "That's an insult, girl, or are you too stupid to understand when somebody calls you poor, dumb, and underprivileged?"

"It's not an insult," I said, trying not to sound superior,

72

though to be truthful, that's how I already felt. My suitcase was only partially packed, but mentally I was already gone from Detroit. Escape was right around the corner, days, not weeks, off. I was scheduled for orientation at Mount Holyoke College, in Massachusetts.

My God. Freedom!

For those fine days of anticipation, not even Josefine had a chance to enter my head. I was filled to bursting with my first real sense of self. I'd done so well already, hadn't I, just scoring high on the test? I'd proved I was much much better than I'd expected—look at my school placement. I'd shown Mom she hadn't been wrong after all, choosing me to replace her own daughter, Caroline. I must have special qualities, now coming to light, and finally, after years of sacrifice, she'd be proud of me.

My last two days home Mom got quiet and withdrawn. Not talking or even fussing, just downcast and morose. One night she kissed me on the forehead—something she hadn't done in years—her eyes vague and distressed and bleary. But when I tried to put my arms around her, impulsive and filled with sudden hope, she went to her room, quickly, and locked her door and didn't come out for the rest of the night.

I was away for eight weeks, the fastest of my life. No time for any lasting relationships, but I was trying to find *myself* so that was just as well. It was the first time I'd experienced total freedom from the specter of Louise. It was the first time in my life that I could hope to be taken at face value, without fear of her sudden, threatening appearance to demean and embarrass me in front of new friends.

At Mount Holyoke, for those eight weeks of orientation, all that anyone knew about my private life were the facts and fictions I personally dished out, and what I told was innocuous and tailored toward an image exactly like everybody else's.

73

Dad came out to visit me at Mount Holyoke. I met him, bursting with pride in my surroundings and myself. Then I had two weeks back home before leaving for my first term at Concord.

I was filled with new resolutions. I no longer desired a false fantasy life. I was determined to enhance myself in every way, first and foremost in my relationship with Mom. If I could tell her how full of vision and excitement I felt, the cold barrier between us would certainly crack. She'd understand how much I wanted her love and how hard I'd work for her approval. How desperately I wanted to live up to her expectations and be perfect.

I went to her in her room. She'd been spending more and more time there, alone.

"I feel—all new," I said. "I feel like a clean new slate. I feel like I can be anything I really want, like nothing can stop me from making it all the way. You'll be proud of me!" I vowed, staring at her though painful, unshed tears, taking a faltering step closer, recalling that single brief kiss before I'd left. Fantasizing that this time she might even put her arms around me and hold me for a minute.

Finally, she met my eyes. She stared at me, unmoving. After a while, her face seemed to go blank. Still, I waited, hope dying hard, until finally, nothing for it, I left her room in silence.

Concord Academy was everything I could have dreamed. Quiet, almost stereotypically scholarly, and steeped in tradition so consistent and intense I was tempted, at first, to think it was a fake.

Mount Holyoke had prepared me for the initial sense of dislocation. But Mount Holyoke was only an eight-week orientation. From the moment I arrived at Concord and set my suitcase down in my room, I knew I was on-stage again, out of my element—whatever that was—and in danger of fouling this great chance up.

I couldn't afford to make mistakes. I couldn't let these people see the countless flaws I believed I carried everywhere I went. It would be deadly for them to judge me different, too—and it wasn't the obvious difference of color or background that I feared.

What hounded every thought in those first whirlwind days was the terror of being unmasked, of being found undeserving, as Louise had always told me I was. Of being forced, through this discovery, to stand apart, branded by my failure to fit in with anybody or anything. It would be a continuation of all the situations of my life. Like the barrier between me and the kids at the military school in Omaha—after all, they had real parents; I was adopted. Like the chasm separating me from the neighborhood kids in Detroit. I'd never felt even a minimal sense of sameness with those streetwise girls.

My experience at juvenile hall had further set me apart. How many girls my age would I meet in a decent environment who could possibly relate to that?

And now, Concord. The ultimate. How could I hope *not* to be left out?

I tried telling myself that any rejection that came would stem from prejudice, because I was black, one of only four black girls at Concord—but I quickly found that I couldn't use that easy out. There really was no sense of barriers in that environment because *acceptance* to Concord was the only real matter of importance to anybody.

Rejection, if it came, would originate in my own mind.

The beautiful old house I lived in wasn't a regulation dorm. It was a *real* house with huge rooms for three or four girls. Bunk beds. Wood floors. Furniture characteristic of the Colonial period. A whole different, demanding world.

Perhaps it was that absolute change from everything that had gone before that finally forced a shift in my attitude and made me loosen up. My roommates were quickly "family." Nothing less was possible in that setting. And it was consequently easier than ever in my life to form friendships in this, my first really stable environment.

I could open up a little. I could *be* a friend. I wasn't always looking over my own shoulder for Louise Evelyn.

That's when I started sharing confidences. Selectively, and always with the purpose of fitting in comfortably. I realize now, looking back, that baring the fact of my adoption at that time was really a rejection on *my* part. I was openly refuting any real bond with Louise, and thereby disassociating myself from future craziness on her part. I suppose I was a sympathetic character in this role—the frank, courageous "orphan" struggling for emotional balance. But whatever my perception of myself then, I did feel a deep, serene happiness.

My entire world had changed. This new part I was playing was quickly grafting itself onto reality. I was maturing, more in charge of myself and my day-to-day practical affairs.

I was painfully careful with my money. I realized I could go home to Detroit for Christmas break only if I stayed at school for the Thanksgiving holiday. It would be my first Thanksgiving completely without the family, but since Dad was gone, nothing had been remotely the same, so I scarcely minded.

When one of the other girls invited me to spend Thanksgiving with her family, I felt that this was part of my new adventure and accepted gladly.

Karen's home wasn't far from the school. It was big and sprawling. There were old trees, long sweeps of lawn that would be glorious in spring and summer. Fenced paddocks formed a storybook backdrop, complete with horses.

I set myself to absorb every aspect of the experience, right down to the atmosphere in Karen's house. The easy relationship of her parents with each other and with Karen. Their life-style. I was fully aware that I aspired to a "life-style" which, at that time, meant only something other than the chaos surrounding Mom.

Well, Karen decided I had to learn to ride on that long weekend. And I was all for it, having always enjoyed physical activities. Besides, Mom had indoctrinated me when I was very young: I was to take every good offer, get the most out of it, and internalize the experience forever—I had to make every effort to overcome my bad blood.

The result was my own ingrained belief that life was a full-time, unrestful challenge. I didn't pass too many offers up.

"Keep your back straight," Karen counseled, sitting her own horse with an ease and style I told myself I'd master quickly enough.

That was seconds before my mare shifted from one foot to another, producing a really alarming dislocation that made me sure I was about to hit the mud so far below us both.

"Legs firm," said Karen. Then, more anxiously, "but don't squeeze."

This advice made me tense, which made me hold more tightly to my reins *and* to my horse, which meant hugging her sides with my knees. She snorted, danced sideways, then threw her head and the reins I'd viewed as lifelines were ripped from my grip.

I don't know how I lost the left stirrup, but I did. I grabbed for the mane, but the horse was still skittering and tossing her chestnut head, twisting violently as I put even more pressure on her with my legs to try to keep my seat.

I remember wrenching my back. I don't recall falling, but I do remember the cracking whack when I landed by the mare's neat feet.

"You'll get better at it," Karen said cheerfully, helping me up. I couldn't detect even the smallest note of derision in her voice. And I did get better at it over the next two days, because I was grimly determined not to fail.

Karen's parents took us out to a seafood restaurant the last night of the holiday break. There was a smell of snow in the air, and I felt invigorated and daring. I went through the menu in that high mood, searching out one last experience.

The tables all around us were jammed and pleasantly noisy. A lot of people were wearing paper bibs with pictures of huge lobsters adorning them. Lobster had an aura for me. It had prestige value. My God! Check out the price! And since I'd never confronted a lobster in my life, there didn't seem to be much choice.

"Are you sure," Karen's mother asked me politely, "that you want a whole lobster? They do a wonderful lobster thermidor. . . ." She gazed at me hopefully.

It was like waving a red flag. I dug in my feet and prepared to do battle. I could manage a lobster as well as anyone else. I could *be* anyone I cared to play, unfettered by the restrictions of knowing the limitations of my true heredity.

"I love whole lobster," I said calmly.

The waiter was hovering.

"A two-pounder," I added, thinking it sounded midsized and probably appropriate for a girl my age.

Well, I don't know just exactly what I expected. A nice cut down the center of the shell, I suppose, and the lobster meat all loose and luscious and waiting for me to spear out with my fork. What I got was a whole lobster, exactly what I'd ordered. A huge creature, flopping over all the sides of my plate, and without a single obvious means of entry.

I sat and stared at this offering for a while, and Karen started eating her shrimp, and Karen's parents kept up a determined light conversation, looking everywhere but at me.

After a while, they fell silent. I hardly noticed. I was so totally ignorant of where to begin that I was still staring blankly at my platter.

Finally, I looked up and met Karen's father's eyes. Then his wife's. We all looked at one another, then I grinned—I found I couldn't help it. They were so easy with each other. I deeply envied Karen's relationship with her mother. I knew it wasn't put on for company either. They simply liked one another.

And the friendliness they shared had extended itself to me. They made me feel so "normal," even at embarrassing moments like this. Admitting ignorance wasn't degrading the way it was with Louise.

Besides, since I'd told Karen I was adopted, I was sure nobody expected perfection of me.

The waiter came back and gave me a complete lesson in the dismantling of a whole lobster. It was one of the best meals of my life, so I figured I'd be making lots of use of the knowledge. It made a warm ending to my first Thanksgiving away from home, and I'd succeeded in saving the money necessary to take Christmas vacation with my family.

I flew home for Christmas, dreaming an emotional welcome. I'd never been away from Mom before, except for orientation. She must have missed me this time. She must have felt a little lonely. Wouldn't any mother? It was her first real *chance* to miss me. She'd had time to realize my achievement now and the pride she should have shown in it.

Aunt Ruth's living room was quiet. Grandma hugged me for a long time in silence. Aunt Ruth smiled and told me, half-kiddingly, I'd grown. My mother scowled and said nothing.

I spent my vacation working, making a few dollars as a clerk in a store near home. I'd always worked odd jobs on every vacation for as long as I could recall. My age had never seemed a deterrent to employment—I had no memory of being idle. And Mom always took half of whatever I earned, whether it was a quarter or ten dollars.

79

Of course, things would be different now. I had expenses of my own to handle. Mom couldn't expect half the money this time. I'd been living pinched down to the barest essentials. I needed a small emergency fund, and I hesitatingly mentioned this fact to Mom, hating myself for sounding so apologetic.

But the tone of my voice didn't matter at all. I owed Mom for all her sacrifices. How dare I be so thoughtless and selfish? She expected an *honest* accounting of my holiday earnings.

My trip back to Concord was another escape. As New Year's had finally pulled around, I'd started counting the seconds. That would have been fine if it was a sign I was finally growing up. That I enjoyed my independence and no longer needed Mom.

But the truth of the matter was I did need her. I craved her approval. I didn't begin to imagine we could ever have the sort of mother-daughter relationship Karen enjoyed, but that Thanksgiving weekend *had* given me hope. Karen's family was perfection; I wanted only a token closeness.

I kept thinking, all the way back to school, about my money. I thought, She keeps everything I hand over to her, and when I finally really need it, maybe when I'm twenty-one, she'll hand me a little bankbook with my own name on it, and there'll be all that money—hundreds or even thousands of dollars in it—all saved up. A nest egg, collected over time, not only from my small earnings, but from all her own money she could spare.

I fantasized how thrilled and touched I'd be when she made a shy little speech about wanting to provide something to start me out on the road to independence.

Shy! Louise!

Back at school, the days melded into a full fall semester. Spring semester then, and the warming days, with hours spent reading novels under spreading trees and indulging in adolescent heavy thinking. I did well at sports, and I laughed a lot—I'd never been aware how little laughter there'd been in life.

It was my first true coming of age, there among the Rockefellers and Pillsburys and Cartiers, and old buildings, and history. It was my first absolute happiness. My first freedom.

I was sure nothing on earth could shatter it.

"It can be very unsettling, adjusting to new situations."

David Aloian, the headmaster, was sitting at his desk in his office looking at me kindly, trying to find excuses for my disappointing first-year grades.

"I don't think, though, that you've experienced any great problems of adjustment. That's not your difficulty. It's been the sheer joy of it, hasn't it? Of just being on your own. Here."

This surprised me. I wasn't prepared for understanding on his part when I felt such shame in myself.

Of course, I was no stranger to shame.

"Are you aware, Doris, of how far below expectations your work has been to date?"

I was miserably aware.

"We don't want to send you back to Detroit."

Detroit? That was a sick and desperate thought. He didn't know how right he was; there was no possible way of returning to Detroit.

My God! My mother would kill me! Worse, she'd stare at me and nod, having expected nothing better anyway.

"You've come too far. It would be a grave mistake. It always is a mistake. expecting people with imagination to vegetate."

I felt, suddenly and terribly, the full weight of my failure. I could see, in ghastly detail, all the golden afternoons I'd spent writing gushing letters, reading thrilling novels, play-

81

ing lacrosse, doing Shakespearean theater, rather than studying and proving my scholastic worth.

"I have a suggestion for you."

I looked at him dully. In my heart, I'd already heard the slamming of all the windows *and* doors. I'd screwed up the biggest break of my entire life. I'd justified Mom's worst estimate of my value. I was desperate, miserable, and furious with myself.

"I feel you may do better in another environment—not a lesser environment," he hastened to add, "simply a different environment. One less rigid," he eyed me speculatively, "and old-world. One with a little more give and take. I think you'll flourish with a bit more of the human touch and with your feet flat to the earth."

I was silent. Optimism was almost dead, but if I chose to believe I'd come out of this okay, maybe I actually would. If I believed only the positive best, only the best would have a chance.

"Let me tell you something about Cushing Academy," he settled into a gentle propaganda pose. "Cushing's here in Massachusetts, an excellent school, high honors, select enrollment. Unlike Concord, a coed school. Bette Davis matriculated at Cushing." He grinned slightly, then ran through a roll call of names I knew from the headlines, from the movie page, from the arts as well.

He was offering me an honorable second chance, one I was well aware I hadn't proved I deserved. I snatched it, of course, and promised to make it work, not only to justify his faith in me, but to redeem my own image of myself. I was so damned relieved to have avoided death in Detroit. And if the shadow knowledge dogged me, never to be dispersed, that I'd failed at the first really important thing I had undertaken, well, that had to be lived with. It was fact, after all.

I'd failed to graduate from Concord.

* * *

Two years later, I graduated from Cushing Academy. I don't know why I thought things would be different at home. Still a dreamer . . .

"You should've quit and come home if you couldn't even make up your mind which school you wanted to attend."

Mom's voice was harsh and furious, even on the phone, long-distance. "You should've made space for a deserving child; you never were deserving, Doris!"

I'd never told her the reason for my transfer. No one else had either.

"Don't you understand?" My voice was too thin. I'd been shocked by her attitude; it was totally bewildering and frightening after I'd been away and safe and had let myself forget a little.

"I *have* made it through, and with decent grades, and I can apply to any college I want now. I have a *great* chance of getting accepted if you'll only sign those papers I sent you months and months back! My God, I didn't know that was why I hadn't heard anything. Why didn't you tell me you hadn't filled them out? Without them my applications aren't complete, they won't even start to process them. . . ."

"No."

"What?" My throat kept trying to close and choke me to death.

"I said no," she repeated.

"No?" My hands had gone sweaty and cold.

"No, I won't sign those papers," she grated. "I won't open up my private affairs to every stranger in the street. I won't put my income, what I've got in my bankbook, I won't tell strangers my personal private business. I'm surprised and ashamed of you, Doris, asking and asking and never content with all you've already been given."

I was so appalled I was very near hysteria.

"You don't understand," I clenched my teeth. "The papers are to prove I need financial assistance, they don't mean to poke into your business, all you're doing is saying I'm telling the truth that I can't afford to pay, myself, for a college education. . . ."

"I'm not signing any 'Parents' Confidential Statement,'" she snapped, her teeth grinding.

"They won't consider my application without that last signed form!" I wailed. "Don't you understand . . . ?"

"And don't you sit there and keep telling me what I do and don't understand either, girl. You keep a civil tongue in your head and try for once in life to do as you're told. If you want so much to go to college, then you find a way to go yourself. How many times do I have to tell you, learn to take responsibility for your own life. Don't keep depending on others for the things *you* want!

"I'm not helping you, I've already given you the best years of my life, I've sacrificed and sacrificed for you with never a word of thanks, a gift is a *loan*," she roared, to my utter confusion and distress.

"Mom . . ."

"I won't *hear* another word, I'm not interested in what you *want*, I have my own life to live, it's time I started enjoying myself. . . ."

"Mom, please . . ."

But the line was dead.

The dean of students was Mr. Morley. I felt humiliated, sitting in his neat little office and telling him as much as I could bear about my "little problem."

But I'd come a long way from the secretive child who'd won that fateful scholarship. I'd stopped hiding myself inside my secret, and by making it common knowledge, I'd defused it as well as used it to my own benefit. I'd stepped away from Louise. I'd made myself totally apart. It didn't matter how crazy she was. It had no reflection on who *I* was, myself.

I didn't know if Mr. Morley was aware I was adopted. That this woman who refused to help me with my life wasn't, after all, my "real" mother. I hoped he knew; it would explain her lack of caring. I told him how worried I was and asked him if there was anything he could do to help me.

"It's getting so late, they'll be settling their fall enrollments, won't they?" I stared at him, too anxious to contain myself.

"I don't know," I said grimly, "what's wrong with my mother," and wondered, as I said it, if he found my situation the most repugnant he'd ever dealt with, or if I was just taking it all too seriously, as usual, because I was so afraid of Mom.

But nothing seemed to surprise or appall Mr. Morley. I couldn't guess if this was because he did know of my adoption and attributed Louise's peculiarities to that cause, or whether he'd simply dealt with so many bizarre situations in his career that nothing shook him at all. He was amazingly self-contained and self-confident.

He promised to call my mother. I don't know what he told her, but at the end of the week the signed papers were in my slot. I sent them on and hoped it wasn't too late for the fall.

It was obvious that Josefine wouldn't have humiliated me this way. Would certainly never have jeopardized my future success. Josefine would have been so proud of me for graduating from Cushing. Our relationship would have been the perfect mother-daughter sharing. A way of thinking along the same lines. Personal taste. A perfect understanding.

It wouldn't even have mattered when we fought. Everyone fights occasionally. I would have been secure in the knowledge that we were friends for life. That she cared for me.

I pictured myself showing her all around campus. I viewed college life as a continuation of life at private school but with even more freedom—the freedom of adulthood.

And suddenly, with that image, I thought, why not? Why was it so absurd to imagine actually doing just that? *Doing it.* Not ending with fantasy! The problem was, I had no knowledge of where to start. But other adopted children found their natural parents, and if I really wanted to find Josefine, what could stop me?

I wasn't a small child anymore, huddling beaten on the bedroom floor. With a little more maturity and self-confidence and some necessary contacts to take my sparse facts and turn them into a phone number or an address, I could make my dream reality.

But first, I had to get into college. I was still too helpless. This latest confrontation with Mom, over the papers, had shown me I really wasn't independent. I had to believe my completed application forms weren't now too late. I had things to prove, not only to Louise, but also to Josefine and to myself.

SIX

I WAS ACCEPTED TO Elmhurst College, just outside Chicago, for the fall semester, 1969. My choice of a major seemed obvious at the time. I wanted something highly visible and spectacular—I had to shine. And I'd played so many roles with my mother, trying for the right one, I'd lived so closely with fantasy all my life, that a career as a famous actress presented itself as the reasonable, natural choice.

"Famous" was the bottom line, of course; I had to be famous. How else could I collect the important contacts I'd need to scour Germany for Josefine? Besides, if I failed to excel, how could I possibly prove my worth to *two* mothers who'd rejected me?

Well, college was a disappointment—reality thwarting expectation. It seemed alien and impersonal compared to both Concord and Cushing academies. I'd stopped being

87

"special," though I didn't realize then that a return to the commonplace formed the root cause of my depression.

Of course, I'd fantasized about college life, and the reality wasn't Ivy League heaven. It was relatively modern buildings, plastic classrooms, and intense concentration on subjects that failed to excite me.

My major was Theater and Speech, and I worked at it. I worked, too, at Chicago Planned Parenthood, saving every penny I could. I was finally really on my own, and I should have exulted in the freedom, but inside I hadn't grown up nearly enough. I was only *physically* free. Emotionally, I might never have left Detroit. My memories and self-doubts haunted me.

Just before this turbulent time, I was lucky to find a father-figure trusted from the start. If my own father had been with me for the unsettling years of adolescence, I don't think I'd have needed anyone else. But he wasn't with me. Louise had seen to that.

My meeting with Robert, happening as it did, seemed almost fated the summer before I left Detroit for Elmhurst.

I'd been seeing a boy named Bill for some time—he was the first love of my life. We were very young and silly and immersed in the pleasure of caring for one another, and we weren't always careful, so it shouldn't have been the surprise it inevitably was when my period was late, signaling big trouble.

I panicked totally. I felt so sick at the thought of the consequences if I really was pregnant and my mother found out that I managed to work myself into a state where I was sure I was not only pregnant, but had syphilis as well.

I couldn't confide in our family doctor. He'd go straight to Mom. Then a friend suggested her own doctor, and that's how I met Robert. I saw him and told him my wildest fears, hardly noticing him as a person. It was only when my

88

tests came back negative that Robert became blindingly frank and personal.

"You're too smart to let yourself get into situations like this, Doris. Don't you have anyone to talk to?"

I was feeling wrung out with the relief of learning my worst fears were unfounded, and it didn't seem strange to want to confide in this total stranger. Hesitant and embarrassed, I told him a little, a very little, about my life.

"If I've read your situation correctly, you've been pretty much riding along just hoping for the best, haven't you?"

I suppose that was a fair assessment. I wasn't cool and calculating or even minimally smart about protecting myself against possible problems. The need for safety had been overridden by the immediate pleasure and warmth Bill and I had found in one another, and I suppose I was also rebelling, doing something Louise would hate. Throwing all her direst predictions right back in her face.

But Robert's assessment of my need for a receptive ear was right on the mark. And he was concerned, yet not intrusive—a difficult balance. He was much older than I was, in my parents' age group, not my own. I considered the possibility of calling him or coming back to see him if I really needed advice, but I didn't jump at the thought; I decided to give it time.

When I left to attend Elmhurst, we did communicate occasionally by phone. Neither of us was a letter writer. He was patient and never condescending, and in some manner I've never really understood, these talks with Robert brought me closer in my mind to Dad and to a beginning understanding of his unyielding belief in his own strength through his faith in God. I didn't stop to wonder then why I didn't just *call* my father instead of calling Robert, but thinking about it now, the answer seems obvious.

I loved Dad too much. I didn't want him to worry or

89

know my unhappiness. I couldn't tell him I was drifting. I didn't want him involved in my problems.

One day, I told Robert I was disillusioned with Elmhurst and bored with my course of study.

"Then come home," he said, reasonably.

"I can't." For I had told him enough personal things for him to understand how I felt.

"Will you *feel* you're grown-up and free to be whatever you want to be until you face your worst memories and deal with them honestly?"

But I couldn't go back to Detroit. It was absurd even to entertain the idea. Yet I couldn't deny the sense in his words either. I felt very unsettled. It was a turning point—I saw that clearly. I had to come to a decision and stick to it.

My overriding awareness was of my own bitterness, and I felt I really deserved some explanation for my stormy relationship with Louise. I remember, even now, the stabbing anger distorting everything as I dwelt on the decisions made *about* me *for* me. By Louise, who'd snatched me away from Dad, my only true security. By Josefine, too. Oh, yes, I'd finally matured enough to lose the gloss on Josefine, who'd given me away—the ultimate rejection—whatever the cause.

It was my anger that drove me—that and the endless questions that made me doubt my own worth. These feelings weren't in any way clear then—I was a muddled mass of indecision, discontent, and unhappiness. In that distorted, unfocused state, no single option toward improvement was too bizarre to chance, and so I actually considered a move back to Louise's turf.

That was during my second year of college. I remember telling myself that going home would give me the chance to clean up old business, which meant dealing with Mom. I could cope with it, woman-to-woman, and try to find reasons for the inconsistencies of my life.

I felt I *needed* to understand Louise if I was to have a chance to throw off childhood grief and my dependence on fantasy and make a future for myself.

Maybe it was only natural that so many years away had blended with maturity so that my memories grew convenient. I know that I smiled scornfully at the child Doris, wondering how she could have been so weak-willed and spineless as to let anyone, even her mother, twist her image of herself ass-backward.

It would be very different now. I'd face Louise as an equal. I'd make her understand how much I needed hard answers, and she'd finally have some respect for me.

Besides, I'd been remembering how different Mom had seemed those last days before orientation. How she'd been so depressed, so quiet and withdrawn. I'd romanticized that one light kiss on the head almost as much as I'd romanticized Josefine.

And things had been changing those last two years. Mom had finally rented her own place, a short distance from Aunt Ruth and Grandma. She'd also remarried, a man named John Lee, and it really was the afterthought it seems, an ill-starred relationship that lasted less than a year. Aunt Ruth told me later that John Lee came home one night to find Louise had changed all the locks on him.

The divorce became final in rapid order, no ugliness, no recriminations from anybody.

I was getting all the family business in just this way—long-distance tidbits. I felt lonely and apart and drifting farther and farther away from *any* sense of family. What I *should* have felt was lucky to be out of it.

All this figured in my final decision about moving back to Detroit.

"I could try to get a transfer," I told Robert the next time we talked. "The phone bills would be a lot easier to take," I added, trying to sound lighthearted, which I was not. "But

I'd need to find a place to live first. And I'd need to get a job."

"You can work for me. In the office." He sounded pleased by this inspiration on his part.

In the end, even finding a place to live turned out too easy to ignore. A friend of a friend was looking for someone compatible as a roommate.

So the halfhearted, fearful possibility I never believed in had snowballed into something I clearly recognized as accomplished fact. And sooner or later, I'd have to make the announcement to my mother. I decided it was easier long-distance.

"You slut," Mom screamed, scorching the phone lines from Chicago to Detroit. "Do you think I can't see your true motives? It's some man, isn't it? Don't think I haven't got you figured inside out! You're a whore, Doris, blood always tells, and you'll never be anything else!"

I could have taken the time to rethink it, of course. I hadn't told Robert I'd decided to accept his offer of a job. I hadn't sealed the arrangement with my prospective roommate, Dorothy. I hadn't even started the paperwork for a transfer from Elmhurst to Wayne State. But I'd made up my mind that I couldn't keep running. Keeping clear of Louise was my greatest act of cowardice. It was time to face the pain and learn how it had started.

Dorothy knew nothing about my problems at home. Her concerns were more immediate.

"You givin' any man a key to this apartment?"

"No key."

"What privileges, then?" That had a decidedly nasty ring to it, but after all, we were just getting to know one another; you had to overlook things in the beginning.

"Privileges?" I murmured.

She folded her arms, eyeing me with open derision.

92

"Look, Dorothy." I sighed. "It's exactly what I told you. No overnights. No key. No privileges. No special man, at least not right now."

I really meant that. I didn't want any cluttered relationships. What I needed was to straighten out the relationships of my childhood, but that wasn't Dorothy's frame of reference, and I don't think she ever believed I was serious.

"Can I borrow your car, Dorothy?"

"What for?"

"I thought I'd run over to visit my grandmother. I've been here two weeks and I haven't been down to the house yet to see her."

Dorothy took her usual long time deciding. That was Dorothy about everything; in fact, she reminded me a lot of Louise Evelyn. She never performed acts of friendship gracefully, preferring me to know just how much she was sacrificing. I didn't understand that. I'd never loved anything I owned enough to sacrifice a chance for a relationship. For me, at that time, acceptance and love were everything.

Already it wasn't working, Dorothy and me.

Finally though, she dangled the keys in front of my nose and set her hips aggressively.

"Okay, Doris, I'll lend you my car. But let me tell you first, it's not something I enjoy. The last time I was nice enough to loan my car to my old roommate, she got it hit. She totaled my car, damn it! So I'll loan you my car to go visit your grandmother, but if you get one little mark on it, I swear, girl, I'll *kill* you!"

I didn't call my grandmother first, figuring to surprise her. It was early Sunday morning. I parked the car at the curb, crossed the walk, climbed to the second floor, and tapped on the door. Grandma's voice called out from back

93

in the kitchen. I hesitated, then walked in. Everybody else did.

My mother stood in the living room.

It jolted me, coming face to face with her so suddenly and unexpectedly. We stared at one another, silent. We hadn't spoken since I'd called to tell her I was moving back to Detroit. She hadn't welcomed me home. Of course not.

"So there you are," she finally said, not looking into my eyes. Feet flat though, and still. One good sign. Strange, that it didn't matter that I was nineteen-plus, not nine. It didn't matter that I was taller than she was now, and that I was a grown woman. It didn't matter that it was absurd to feel the old surge of fear. These things were ingrown and still made me need to urinate.

I moved a little back. She stood hunched, as if she was hurting, her breath coming too fast, her eyes squinting. Her arms were tight around herself, then suddenly, she straightened. A hardness crept into her face. When she spoke, her tone was a whiplash.

"Why the hell did you have to come back to Detroit, Doris?"

I just stared at her dumbly. I don't think it had ever occurred to me that she was *relieved* when I'd left for Concord. That she wanted some distance between her pain and its source, no matter why the pain existed. Hadn't she left my father, whom I was sure she'd still loved? She'd put distance between them when their relationship started to cause her pain, rather than finding and treating the source.

"Why did you come back?" she persisted, taking a step forward. "To shame me, to embarrass me in front of my friends? I thought you'd grown up. I thought you'd learned enough sense. . . ."

The accusation was miserably unfair and untrue, and I hadn't the time or the desire to think about her motives or

94

to care to save her feelings. I felt cold and wounded and, oddly, ashamed of *her*.

"I never did anything to shame you . . . ," I said as flatly and emotionlessly as I could. "And I don't intend to have one of these stupid shouting matches you're building up to either."

She stared at me, then laughed sharply. "You *are* shame, girl. Don't you even know what you are?"

But I'd already spent the years of my life wondering what I was. Wondering and imagining all the possible goods and evils I'd inherited from that shadow-woman Mom hated so much.

Josefine.

"I'm sorry," I said, incomprehensibly and inadequately, and turned, fumbling, to go. "Please tell Grandma I'll come back to see her when she's alone."

And suddenly, without warning, she was flying at me across the room. I saw the swift rush from the corner of my eye, then her fist caught me over my ear and staggered me, and I tripped and nearly fell, and she was all over me, punching me in the head, in the neck, in the chest, and screaming at the top of her lungs.

I threw my arms up over my head, stumbling toward the door. It never occurred to me to hit her back—she was my mother.

"Keep away from that door," she howled. "If you try to leave this house I'll shoot your ass! I have a gun!"

I never doubted the possibility. She was crazy enough to have a gun. It was only that instead of slowing me down, her threat shot me straight out the door.

I ran like hell, down the steps and across to the car. The door was unlocked; I fell inside, banging my elbow a terrific whack. My hands were shaking so badly I couldn't get the key in the ignition slot. It finally jammed in; I gunned up and jerked the wheel around.

Louise Evelyn was racing toward the street, waving her arms.

I took that car away from the curb. I was watching my mother hurtling toward the street, so I didn't pull out far enough, and there was the tearing shriek of mauled metal as Dorothy's beloved Cutlass Supreme grazed the car parked in front.

Then Mom had made it down to the curb and was threatening to jump in front of the car. Daring me to run her over—she'd never know how close I came to doing just that. Then I was past her, missing her by a hair, blinded by hysterics, driving all over the road.

Halfway back to the apartment, I realized my dilemma. My mother was back at one end of my trip, wanting to shoot me for coming back to Detroit, and Dorothy was at the other end, waiting to kill me for smashing the Cutlass Supreme.

I screeched the Cutlass up lopside in front of the apartment building, jumped out and stormed the door, banging wildly and screaming, "Let me in, let me in, let me in!" until Dorothy finally opened up, her eyes popping out of her head.

I threw up all over Dorothy and her nice blue rug.

SEVEN

I WALKED A SPECIAL tightrope. Always. That's my most graphic memory image of myself. Maybe I meant to and climbed up willingly. Maybe I felt I had no personal choice. But from the first time I heard Louise use the term "real mother" when speaking of that unknown, her daughter, Caroline, I was set on a path with improbable goals and no real sense of how to achieve success.

The fact that I was adopted became a twisted misery in my head. I couldn't help a growing sense of rejection as maturity filtered the romantic fantasies of childhood down to something more realistic and less pleasant. If I hadn't been emotionally rejected by Louise, I wouldn't, as a child, have built Josefine into the perfect mother-figure. I believe my need to know would have settled down to a vague and itching disquiet, far removed from what became a biting preoccupation.

Adopted kids, I came to tell myself, bitterly, just naturally have to try harder. They have to pay back all the sacrifices. They have to justify themselves to everybody.

Toward this impossible end of being everything to all people, I should at least have set intermediate goals, but I was just as unsure of my life's direction as anyone my age. I had no detailed plans. Even the ABC Program had been more a matter of luck than design, of being in the right place at the right time.

Up to the time of my decision to return to Detroit, I hadn't been shrewd and calculating—it hadn't been my nature. But I started to feel that I had to protect myself. I was getting too old for irresponsible pigheadedness. I could see so clearly through hindsight what I should have worked out before: that coming home had been the wrong move and that I should have believed what my heart had told me for years: I'd never learn how to earn Louise's love unless I understood her emotional problems.

I felt helplessly driven to discover what was wrong. More than ever before, I knew I had to make her tell me why she'd pushed me away when I'd done everything I could to win her approval and support. I had to know these things for their own sake, it was true, but always, behind everything, was the desperate obsession to discover what *she* knew about Josefine, what information she might have to help me trace my way back to Germany and my roots.

I *had* to. I had no choice. Even now, I don't know why I had no choice.

And I promised myself if I failed utterly with Mom, as I was quite sure I would, I'd find other options, depending on no one but myself.

This much was clear as I started my third year of college, at Wayne State University. I got a student loan and Robert was true to his word, employing me in his office and paying me a weekly salary. I'd promised myself this arrangement would be temporary. I didn't want to have to depend on anybody. It was comforting to know that Robert was there,

98

consistent and trustworthy, but leaning on people I perceived as emotionally stronger than myself struck me as the basest form of immaturity.

I was determined to grow up.

I worked for Robert while looking for something else, and after several months a job at Detroit Planned Parenthood opened up.

It was another period of transition. I forced myself to stop calling on Robert for emotional reassurance. I reassessed everything, including my living arrangements. Dorothy and I shared a genuine chemical dislike for one another, which didn't improve even after I had her car fixed. It wasn't any easier trying to get along with Dorothy than it would have been living with Louise Evelyn.

I started looking for my own apartment.

My fantasies renewed in force, as they always did in periods of insecurity. It was my personal escape from dealing with unhappiness. Josefine lived in these times, despite my growing cynicism. If I could no longer make her perfect, her motives pure, I could at least view her as differently as possible from Louise.

I stopped judging her character, for judgments led to doubts. Instead, I tried to enlarge on my old dreams by imagining the place of my birth. What did it look like? Was it old-world European? A charming village with cobbled streets and that romantic difference in color that I understood different angles of light gave to different countries?

Josefine would live on a narrow street in a little house, alone. I always pictured her alone. I could conjure the atmosphere so easily; it was the very essence of warmth and homecoming. There were small, graceful trees by Josefine's door. A little walled garden. Pretty shutters on the windows—blue, I thought. Everybody who passed had a kind word for Josefine—she was so gentle and quiet and vulnerable.

But no one really knew her. I stressed that to myself. She

was the ultimate mystery woman. People thought she must have had a tragedy in her life, but she kept her grief locked inside, exactly as I would have done.

I colored my thoughts with these wild imaginings—the blight and the privilege of the unhappy adopted child. It was never my natural father who figured in any of this. He didn't seem important because I didn't see him as responsible for my adoption. It was my biological mother who'd always held the key. I'd placed all the answers with Josefine.

She was the natural, obvious focus of the mystery. The only true answer to Louise's cruel taunts—I remember every spiteful word that had threatened my earliest imagined hopes about myself. After all, if Mom was right about Josefine, what did that make me? It was the ever-lurking death of fantasy.

It was time now to keep a sharp eye out for people who might help me search for her. To make finding these contacts a major goal. But exactly what I'd do if I actually found someone was a mystery. After all, there was still the old problem of dealing with Louise.

I was introduced to Ed Woodman just after I started working for Planned Parenthood. Ed was older, soft-spoken, gentle, and vain. He told me he was thirty-seven, and by looks it was barely possible, but his manner was more mature and his reminiscences a dead giveaway.

I didn't mind his small deception. In the total spectrum of failings I'd already witnessed in my life, vanity wasn't deadly.

Ed had a thriving business in Detroit and Germany—automotive parts and munitions. Here was my first "contact." It was obvious. Ed went back and forth to Germany. Yet, faced with my big chance, I hesitated to tell him about Josefine. I felt I'd be vulnerable once I'd confided. He'd know too much of my feelings. And though I did, eventually, tell him of my own "German connection," I left it there, vague. I never asked him to help me find Josefine.

This forced me to admit I wasn't really sure what I wanted, despite all the fantasies. All my big promises to myself, made conveniently in silence, in the dark, were extensions of old dreams and not a bit more solid. And I could tell myself forever that it was all Louise's fault. That it would be cruel, and dangerous besides, to have her know I was looking for Josefine.

But the true problem, as I was starting to see, lived deep-rooted in me. I was *afraid* to find Josefine.

Ed told me he'd had an affair with a German woman and that they'd had a child—Eddie. He told me he was fascinated with all things German, so I suppose it was only natural for that fascination to extend itself to me—a black, half-German woman.

I had nearly two years of school to go when Ed asked me to move into his house. I'd lost credits when I'd transferred from Elmhurst to Wayne State, and my academic requirements were making it impossible to work enough hours to support myself. I cared enough about Ed to consider his offer seriously. He represented a certain degree of security to me, but even so, a warning bell dinged against giving up my half of Dorothy's apartment. Living with Ed for a while was fine, but not if it meant losing my independence. Hadn't life with Mom taught me never to depend on anyone but myself? Never to be vulnerable?

I moved in with Ed but kept on searching for an apartment I could rent without a roommate.

The notes started appearing on my car windshield a few weeks later. They were handwritten and unsigned and were thick with Louise Evelyn's style.

Doris,
I know you're in there.

That was the first one, and I nearly just threw it away, thinking it was an advertisement. They came at frequent intervals after that; I opened each one with foreboding mixed with amusement.

Doris,

How could you? He's an old man. Disgusting!

That made me coldly angry. I resolved not to read any future notes, but, of course, curiosity got the better of me.

Doris,

You can always tell a man's age by the rings around his neck. That one's fifty-five if he's a day!

I laughed at that one—a single small laugh in a wilderness of incomprehension. I think that's when I first became aware of the force of opposing needs driving Louise. Self-protection, thrusting me out of her life. Something else, then, nameless, making desperate little attempts to pull me back in, but without spoken commitments.

Ed told me one morning that Erica, the mother of his child, was coming to the States, from Germany, and bringing little Eddie. He was obviously thrilled at the thought of seeing his son, and I sensed something else in his manner— a nervousness I could interpret only as desire to be alone. That didn't bother me much. I'd finally found a little apartment I could afford on Willis Avenue. It was in a pretty rough area of Detroit, but it was mine, my symbol of independence, and I'd been planning a housewarming.

I moved my things out of Ed's big house to give him room in his old relationship.

The night of my party, Ed was very late. I phoned the

house to see if he'd left yet. A woman answered the phone—Erica, she said. Oh yes, she knew about me, Ed had told her, he was on his way. It was so very civilized that I was encouraged to ask how long she and her little boy were planning to stay.

"Why, until after the divorce is finalized."

The phone line hummed while my head tried to make sense of what she'd just said.

She laughed slightly. "Didn't Ed tell you we are married, Doris?"

So Ed couldn't be trusted either. Oh, he came clean when I confronted him later that night. He was so hangdog, so terribly distressed that I should have learned this truth so baldly from Erica rather than tactfully and with his interpretation of the facts. His explanations were too glib, I knew that at the time. But I'd gotten stuck in this relationship and wasn't emotionally prepared to tell him to walk. For someone so determined to be independent, I seemed to have an incredible amount of trouble breaking things off.

Besides, I could rationalize my procrastination in this matter. I had my apartment, my little lifeline. I could try it again with Ed as soon as Erica and her child left, and if I didn't care for the way things worked out, I could always come back to my own place.

Well, things didn't really sort themselves out as quickly or neatly as that. In the end, I stayed with Ed for nearly two years, and for no earthshaking reason other than my desire for the security that comes with being needed. That requirement—to be needed—transcended a lot. Ed was stubborn and overbearing. He could be incredibly mean. He was verbally abusive and didn't seem to mind embarrassing me in private or in public either. These traits grew more overt as time continued to pass, a build-up born of over-familiarity.

Even so, I was firmly stuck in my rut. I needed some impetus to get myself out of the relationship and back to depending solely on myself. I realize now that I still needed to see my worth reflected in the love of another human being.

I'd been making it a habit to return to my apartment twice a week to dust, look in the mailbox, and be alone with my thoughts. I was far from complacent, but I kept telling myself I was reasonably comfortable and safe and that was enough.

Ed took a business trip to Germany a year after his divorce, in the winter of 1971. He took the opportunity to get Erica pregnant again, a fact she didn't keep to herself.

I finally had my impetus. I packed up my bags and literally fled Ed's house, remembering my mother's exact words as she packed and raved, leaving Dad and Omaha.

"Never leave yourself dependent on any man. A woman always needs a fallback position. Men can't be trusted, no matter how good they seem. They always end up a bitter disappointment."

Ed turned up on my doorstep and begged me to come back. When I asked him to leave, he planted himself there, by the door, and destroyed what was left of my respect for him.

A good chunk of disastrous innocence was finally gone. Whatever the result, I was back to single living.

I changed my major from Theater and Speech to Mass Communications. It had suddenly become clear that an acting career was just one more pointless fantasy. It was time to be more realistic about my life, and a job in the media seemed challenging and on-track.

In my last year of college, I started hanging out with anyone interested or involved in the media. I didn't restrict myself—that covered radio, television, journalism. There was always a professor who knew somebody who knew somebody else, or a fellow student taking a relevant elective.

Contacts. A new peer group. A definite step forward toward finding Josefine if I ever matured enough to master my own fears. A very big "if" even then, though now it seems very hard to believe. Why was I so afraid?

I hadn't totally abandoned all thought of an acting career, but I knew that the role of the dewy starlet wasn't for me. Poverty didn't become me. Acting might lie somewhere far up the road, but right then, very young and without any experience, what I wanted was a field where I could learn to promote myself. Something hugely noticeable, which couldn't possibly be yawned away or ignored, where Doris McMillon had half a chance to become a household word.

I didn't care whom I was trying to impress. I knew, even then, that the answer was difficult and devious. Part of it was vindication in terms of Louise. It was saying, "See! You chose right. You should know enough to be proud of me!" Part was directed at the shadow of Josefine. "See," that part said, "how wrong you were to abandon me?"

I started talking about my desire to get into radio or television broadcasting in the hope that if enough people ultimately knew, something might connect. I felt very strongly that the timing would come right if I was patient and determined enough.

James Reese was the news director at WJLB, one of the black radio stations in the city. One evening, at a small party, I asked him half-kiddingly if his station needed a newswoman to give it tone and class, and he told me, half-seriously, that his station wasn't ready for a woman but that he'd keep his ear to the ground for me.

Late July 1971. I'd been out job-hunting. Career moves were fine, but I had to eat. I'd just about decided to take a job as a reservationist for American Airlines at eight thousand dollars a year. It was that or doing secretarial work, which I loathed, for an ad agency.

Jim Reese called.

"WJR's looking for a new personality, Doris. It can't hurt to get your own two cents in. If you'd like to make a tape, come down to JLB in the morning and I'll help you put one together for an interview."

It's probably a good thing I didn't know WJR's reputation. That Jim didn't mention it was a powerhouse station. That I'd never heard of the excellence of its news department. That I didn't know even my Dad, in Omaha, could sometimes pick up JR's fifty thousand watt clear signal.

Jim tore some wire copy and let me run it through. Over and over, trying it in a multitude of different ways until I had something he said was interesting. He put the tape together and sent me off on my own, and I called WJR and requested an interview.

Then I went out and bought a wig to cover the Afro I'd been sporting. What Jim *had* mentioned was that WJR was a white station and very conservative. I was willing to make some temporary changes because I wanted a true shot. I'd made up my mind I wasn't about to be dismissed because my hair looked militant and made people nervous.

The news director at WJR was Dave White. He interviewed me and listened to my tape and told me I read very well. He was openly pleased I was lacking a "black accent." He was openly sorry I had no field experience.

"There are a couple of routes you could consider," he said. "On-the-job training, if you could find a station willing to invest the time and take the chance.

"Or you could try something like the Columbia University fellowship program in journalism. That might be the logical next step if you're serious about trying your hand in this business. There aren't many long-lived shortcuts."

"You feel," I ventured, figuring I had nothing to lose, "that WJR wouldn't be interested in taking the chance on a new personality?"

He smiled slightly. "I didn't say that. But I don't have an answer for you now. I'll get back to you in a few days. Meanwhile, consider what I said about taking a course specifically geared toward broadcast journalism."

106

Well, I pretty much decided it was a classic rejection: Don't call us. We'll call you. We've got your application. But two days later, Dave White called. They'd decided, he said, despite my lack of experience, to hire me and train me at WJR. He asked me how much I expected to make and, with the thought of the airline reservationist job in mind, I stuttered out my first thought—eighty-five hundred dollars. Later, when I learned that other women in my position were starting at ten and eleven thousand, I made the vow never to undersell myself again, and I stuck to it.

I started that August 1971, at WJR. I wore my conservative wig for the first three days on the job. Then one morning I felt like the ass I was and combed out my Afro. Nobody at WJR died of shock.

I felt myself slide smoothly into the life, despite a terrible schedule that could have cut short my career aspirations literally overnight. I had a new peer group that immediately felt natural. It was another one of those learning situations I'd been seeking out for some time. I knew I was on-target. This wasn't a false start.

It was at a black broadcasters' meeting early on in my new job that I met Margaret Gasby, who was to become my best friend in life. At the time, she was working for WGPR radio, and I was there, at the meeting, with my friend and neighbor Loretta Fuller. Loretta and Margaret had shared some classes at Wayne State, and Loretta introduced Margaret and me to one another.

We ran into each other again in a Mass Communications class at Wayne State. I guess our personalities just meshed. We shared the same basic outlook on life. We both considered ourselves ambitious. We shared the direction of our thoughts—something that had never happened to me before. We could finish each other's sentences with ease when we'd only known each other a few months.

I invited Margaret to my apartment, interested in her re-

107

actions. I'd moved to a much better area of Detroit when I'd gotten the job at WJR. The rent was higher, but I could just manage it, and I clearly understood the need to make the image fit the desire. Toward that goal, I'd decorated my rooms unrelentingly in my own style—a mixture of inherent preference for classic elegance and a helpless compulsive neatness instilled by Mom.

I'll never forget Margaret's expression as she stared at my big brown wing-backed early American couch and the orange chair keeping it company.

"Well?"

She pushed her hands through her hair, hesitated, then grinned.

"Girl, don't *ask* me for an opinion this early. I mean, you're dealing with somebody who's been seriously into chrome for years. . . ."

We were very much alike, and yet totally different. We fit together comfortably and neatly, balancing our talents and our preferences. Margaret was outspoken about everything, which included my habits. No one else had ever mentioned my quirks, but I guess with Margaret, nothing was off-limits from the start.

"I have never," she stated flatly, "actually seen closets like yours." She reached out and touched a blue blouse, then gazed disbelieving at the rest of the closet's contents. "You've got everything here in color order. Not only that," she said, her voice rising a little, "my God, girl, they're in categories, too, aren't they?"

Well, of course they were. All the pink blouses together, for example. All the black pants. How else did you arrange clothing?

It had never occurred to me until that moment that my way of dealing with things was rote and neurotic. Routines hammered in by my mother, of course. There was only one possible way of doing anything. I'd never regarded this or any other aspect of my behavior as compulsive. And since

108

I'd never felt I could really confide in anyone about Mom, I'd never had the opportunity to talk over my *perceived* problems either.

But I thought I might someday confide in Margaret, if I could just overcome the dread of being vulnerable. No sudden moves. We'd either last, or we wouldn't.

I spent a year and nine months learning to be a reporter. I was designated an intern for the first twelve months. It was JR's requirement that I finish my education at Wayne State, which meant working insane hours.

From the beginning, I went out with the reporters. I knew I had to earn getting on the air. JR already had their token black reporter. His name was Cliff Mosley.

I went everywhere with the reporters, and the skills came naturally. Not like some of the courses I'd battered my way through at private school and college. The business reporter, Bill Curnow, took me under his wing. He was kindhearted and had a great sense of humor and seemed genuinely interested in my learning the business.

Rod Hanson did the investigative stuff. Gene Fogel, Oscar Frenette—they all did their best to get me well-grounded in every aspect of the business.

In this warm, supportive climate, I learned how to report and how to write up the stories. I started to help the guys rewrite their wire copy. I got the hang of it quickly; it had started being fun. I'd go out with the others to cover a story, come back and write it up myself for the practice, hoping it would pay off. I learned to edit tape for radio. All the skills of radio reporting.

After months of this same exact routine, I felt I wasn't progressing. I wanted desperately to get on the air and begged Dave White to give me a chance to do a newscast, but he insisted I wasn't ready.

JR had both AM and FM stations. The FM featured elevator music and one-minute news capsules. These capsules had become a real chore for the reporters, who had too many other responsibilities already, just reporting. I started practicing writing up the capsules, and reading them as well, which led to my first big break since landing the job itself.

Rod Hanson could no longer make the time to do the capsules. He saw how eager I was to try and asked Dave to give me a shot. I got my chance, then, and I came across well, and the capsules were mine.

One morning, all the rhythms at the station were out of whack. Or maybe it was just poor planning, but whatever the cause, that particular morning there were literally no warm bodies in the newsroom. Everybody alive except Doris McMillon had gone out on a story. No one was left to write the newscast or go on the air to report it.

It was my great opportunity to anchor. And Dave, in a corner, didn't have many options. He let me do five newscasts, back to back, an awesome task for an untried newcomer alone in the booth for the first time. Cliff Mosley, racing out to yet another story, took a minute to show me how to punch up all the buttons in the booth and get the mike going; then he, too, vanished.

My one-year anniversary at WJR. I was off and running. I knew at the end of that incredible day that this was what I wanted. I was permanent after that, no longer an intern, and I even got a raise in salary, up to $11,500.

My schedule, if anything, worsened. I might come in at ten in the morning on Friday and leave at six, then come back Saturday at four in the morning and leave at ten A.M. Back then that same night at eleven to work through the overnight shift until seven or eight Sunday morning.

It started making me crazy. I couldn't adjust. I had a tendency to need sleep on a regular basis and an apparent inability to move that sleep to daylight hours.

This lack of adaptability was nearly my downfall.

Three in the morning! Overnight shift! The five-minute

network news came on the air, and I was supposed to follow with local news. I was exhausted that night, and I fell asleep. That's how the station engineer found me.

"Doris?" I woke slowly, not knowing why I was hunched over a desk or why this man was shaking me.

"Don't you think it might be a good idea," he asked calmly, "if you got yourself down to the studio?"

I blinked at the clock and left my chair in a desperate rush, grabbed for what I thought was my script and raced down the hall. I came gasping onto the air, looking frantically down at my papers to find I didn't have all the news, not nearly enough for a three-minute newscast. Just sports and weather—it's very hard to make sports and weather stretch when you're not even sure what you're reading and you're still only half-awake.

I prayed nobody influential was listening. It seemed like a fairly good bet. It *was* three in the morning. Unfortunately for me, one of our local black city councilmen not only was listening but also decided to cream me for inefficiency. He called Dave White the next morning with a full report, and if it hadn't been my first screw-up, my career might have ended that night.

There was a note from Dave on the desk the next time I came to work.

Doris,

No more breathless and belated appearances! Please.

I graduated from Wayne State University in June of 1974, and back into the dark side of my life danced Louise Evelyn.

EIGHT

MOM MARRIED JAMES MURPHY during my last year of college. He was a quiet man and strong, the sort of personality that should have calmed her down, but then, Dad never had, and I wasn't exactly a front row observer of this third marriage either.

I made it a point to visit Grandma whenever I could, but my schedule was so packed with JR and school that the visits were relatively few. Each time I went to see her, I considered asking about Louise. About what she'd been like as a girl—her personality and temper and relationships. Most of all, I wanted to know if Mom had always had these violent mood shifts.

I needed confidence so badly. I wanted desperately to believe I wasn't the cause of all the unhappiness. I could live with the knowledge I'd just happened along in the middle of some lifelong crisis of Mom's. I could rationalize all the misery away if I knew that whatever plagued Mom was inherent in *her* and not a reaction to me.

Of course, I never did ask Grandma anything. Our closeness wasn't that sort. She was warm and showed great affection and interest in my experiences, but there was a core of privacy I thought I knew better than to invade. I believed she'd pull back if I trespassed on her personal memories.

I was afraid of more rejection. And I knew Grandma wouldn't or couldn't help me anyway—she couldn't even help herself. I'd witnessed my mother's marginal scorn more times than I could count when the two of them were talking. Another mother-daughter relationship with all the good parts lacking. Grandma never showed if the disrespect hurt. She simply closed herself up.

And whenever I did visit and Mom was there, the atmosphere was miserable.

It didn't require a high IQ to learn the wisdom of avoiding any mention of Dad when my mother was in the room. Dad had also remarried, just after the divorce, which gave Mom a brand-new foe, Lena, Dad's second wife. Mom convinced herself that Lena was responsible for all her problems, and when Lena committed the unpardonable sin of giving Dad a baby son, well . . .

In Mom's vicious hatred for Lena was the mirror image of her hatred for Josefine.

Mom had honed in on Lena even before the divorce was final. There'd been one all-out confrontation, when we'd gone back that last time to Omaha. Mom had tried to beat up Lena, outside the church. She finally had to accept the clear fact that her marriage was over, and since she couldn't have Dad, she needed some convenient outside cause. It didn't matter to Mom that it was she herself who'd threatened Dad, and separated from him, and left no other possible option but the finality of divorce.

113

Even when I was relatively young, immersed in my own problems and escaping into dreams of Josefine, I realized that Mom didn't understand what she'd done. Why she'd thrown away what she loved.

But I never applied those concepts to myself. I was too deeply involved to be able to rationalize such a self-destructive tendency in Louise toward me—her adopted daughter.

And whenever I thought of her hatred for Lena, it triggered all my memories of her hatred for Josefine. I heard her ranting voice again in my thoughts—indelible memory. I felt the choking bond *she'd* laid around me through her endless taunts: I was just like my natural mother; blood always tells.

In this way, she'd driven me from her arms toward the shadow of Josefine. It was unnatural. It was sick. The older I grew, the more I understood the extent of such mental instability.

It wasn't unreasonable that I came to believe her capable of great violence if I actually tried to find Josefine, but I realize now that I used that belief as a convenient crutch, a means of putting off a decision to pursue my dreams. I was afraid of Louise, but I was terrified of the end of all my fantasies.

In June of 1974, I was about to graduate college. I'd worked so hard, it was all I could think of. The personal problems of my parents and their new families were secondary. I was proud of myself for having survived my wicked work/school schedule. I was still young enough to think my own pleasure should surmount everything, which is why I honestly believed it was my right to invite Dad and his family to graduation.

We'd talked as often as we could, long-distance. It had left me with a sense of helpless loss, never seeing him. Once I'd gotten it in my head that he *had* to come to graduation,

114

no reason would have stopped me from calling him and asking him.

The line hummed all the way between Detroit and Omaha before he answered me.

"I don't know if I can do it," he finally said. "Finances are tight. I'm really sorry, Doris. I hope you know in your heart how much I want to see you in your moment, but there's no reasonable way to afford it , . ."

I'd put money away working all those crazy hours and not having time to spend it, so I suggested sending him whatever he'd need to bring himself, Lena, and their young son to my graduation ceremony. It took a lot of talking to bring him around. He didn't want to spend my savings, but I got carried away, explaining how important it was to me to have a sense of family, to feel whole again, as I hadn't felt since childhood and the divorce. To have my father with me.

When he finally agreed, I felt marvelous. I called Aunt Ruth to tell her my news, too damn full of myself, too blind to everyone else's realities.

The ceremony was held in Cobo Hall. It was an arena— sporting events were held there. Even so, it wasn't big enough for Mom *and* Dad and Lena.

Just before the ceremony, Mom stalked into the hall with her husband, Mr. Murphy. I was talking to my neighbor and friend, Loretta Fuller. Margaret wasn't there. Our friendship was deepening, but it hadn't yet reached the stage of invitations to special affairs. Loretta and I, on the other hand, had been comfortable with one another for the past year.

My gown was hot, my cap weighed a ton, and the tassel kept tickling, but none of that mattered the least bit; I felt high and pleased with life until I turned to see Mom's bloated features. She hadn't looked like that in a very long time, and I'd hoped never to see it again.

My heart started slogging.

"Where are they?" she whispered, eyes sliding this way and that, settling on strange faces and bouncing frenetically back. The families and friends of the other graduates made walls of solid, shifting flesh.

"I'm gonna kick that bitch's ass all over this place," she hissed. "Cobo Hall's not big enough for all of us. You go find them, tell that whore somebody's got to leave, and it's not gonna be Louise Evelyn!"

"Mom, please . . ." My eyes felt like they were starting out of my head. Surprise! Surprise! I'd done it to myself again.

I hurried away to sit with my group, praying for a miracle. There were speeches I didn't hear, and finally I got my diploma. All the while all I could think of was Mom sitting stiff and clenched beside Mr. Murphy, while far over in the hall Dad, Lena, and their son were temporarily protected by a comforting crush of thousands of strangers. I kept wondering if it was possible to keep them from meeting. After the ceremony, I was going out to dinner, with Dad and his family, and Loretta, and Tom Turner—a dear friend and Detroit AFL-CIO bigwig. I'd have to say goodbye to Mom and Mr. Murphy, thank them for coming, then beat a fast retreat from the building.

At the end of the ceremony, inside the maddening crush of haphazardly wandering strangers, the diverse members of my family all met in a whirlwind outside one of the doors of Cobo Hall, exactly as if it was destined.

Mom advanced ominously. She knew my dinner plans—I hadn't hidden anything. It hadn't occurred to me until that moment that Mom might well consider Detroit her own personal turf and doubly resent Tom's presence at a dinner with my father and Lena. It would have made Mom's evening to be the one invited out with Tom—she loved the idea of celebrity.

I burst into frantic speech, figuring if I talked fast and furiously enough, she wouldn't be able to say anything, and Lena stood back watching her come, with her own dark eyes narrowed dangerously.

"I'm going out to dinner now," I babbled, "so I'll talk to you tomorrow. It was nice, wasn't it . . .? We've gotta go or we'll miss our reservations. . . ."

She grabbed onto my sleeve, other hand on her hip, lip thrust out mutinously.

"Oh, no, you're not going to dinner," she said emphatically. "You're takin' me home since I came all this way to see *your* graduation."

I glanced behind her, but Mr. Murphy was gone.

"James went home," Mom announced, grinning balefully.

I stared at her. "He went home?" I heard my voice climb in disbelief. Hell, I'd just seen him, hadn't I? I mean, he'd brought her; he'd sat through graduation.

"I *sent* him home," she snapped, showing her teeth.

"You mean you wanted to start trouble," I corrected her unwisely, growing grim and furious, seeing my special night going down the tubes while Dad vanished from my life as he had before and I had the dubious pleasure of placating my mother.

Loretta, beside me, had never seen Mom in a rage. In truth, she'd seen her seldom. I hadn't made it a habit to invite Mom to my apartment. I couldn't trust her moods and I didn't want my possessions in ruins. Loretta, therefore, went soft about the situation. She pictured Mom a lonely woman who wanted some time with her newly graduated daughter and who felt, understandably, left out of the picture. And I'm not saying Loretta was wrong in her assessment. Only in her "logical" suggestion.

"Look, Doris, why don't we just run her home, make her feel wanted, you know?" she whispered. "Spend a few minutes thanking her for coming, let her tell you how proud she is of you—you have to understand how she must feel thinking you'd rather spend the time with your father, how sad that must make her.

"Tom can go ahead with your dad and his family to dinner, and when we get your Mom home and tucked up nice," she grinned, "we can go join them. We won't miss anything and you'll have done your good deed for everybody."

It would have made perfect sense if we were discussing anybody but my mother.

Unfortunately, there was nothing else to do. I couldn't just leave Mom standing there, and with Mr. Murphy gone, there was no way for her to get herself home—a fact she well knew. It would have put me totally in the wrong to go along with Dad and Lena and my friends, as planned. She'd maneuvered me beautifully.

I felt myself going cold with fury.

I told Dad we'd meet him at the restaurant, then started away from Cobo Hall. I didn't speak to my mother; I couldn't even look at her. I could hear her panting behind me while Loretta strode along ahead, and we were waiting to cross the boulevard when, without warning, Mom jumped forward and punched me in the face.

Cars hurtled past. The boulevard was wicked. Horns blared in a passing whine as I stumbled forward, unbalancing. Loretta snatched at me and missed, and I felt her fingers ripped from my sleeve and I caught myself, whirling to face my mother in the middle of the street. That's when I lost the last of my inhibitions.

I was twenty-three. A grown woman, not a baby. I was a professional in this town, working for one of the best radio stations in the country. I felt ludicrous and at a disadvantage

118

in my cap and gown, with the tassel flipping forward and backward and a crazy woman trying to pound me.

Mom punched me again, this time in the chest, and horns blared, brakes screeching. Someone shouted derisively at us in a roar of exhaust, and I degenerated to the desperate level of juvenile hall.

For the first time in my life, I squared off and punched my mother back with all my strength, my graduation robes flapping. We fought our way across the boulevard, all the way to the parking lot, up and down the aisles with me gasping and her grunting and Loretta crying and murmuring and other people trying not to notice us. Through it all, in the midst of all this absurdity, I kept trying to remember where I'd left the damn car, and then suddenly it was there, in front of me.

I grabbed at the door handle. Christ! I'd forgotten to lock it!

That meant the passenger side . . .? It was too awful to contemplate.

I fell onto the driver's seat to find Mom climbing in from the other side, puffing and panting and squaring off all over again. Loretta had been first in, much to her own regret, for the car was a two-door, and Loretta, diving for cover in the back seat, was trapped by my mother and me up front.

I threw myself back against the driver's seat door, fending off Mom's fists.

"Get out of my car or I'll throw you out," I screamed.

"Just take her home, Doris," Loretta gabbled, as Mom set herself firm in her seat.

I was only too well aware of the emptiness of my threat. I didn't believe I was physically capable of throwing her out on the lot. Filled with helpless fury, I slammed the car out into traffic, out onto the John C. Lodge Expressway, gunning the engine, racing for Mom's house, my eyes pinned to the road and seeing nothing but the degradation of all the years since childhood. I wanted only one thing in life—to get rid of Louise Evelyn, no matter what it took.

"I'm not *goin'* home," Mom spat at me.

I snaked my lips back from my teeth and didn't bother to argue it with her.

"You think I'm kidding?" she yelled and reached across and punched me again, over the right eye, with me doing seventy on the expressway.

Loretta, in the back, started wailing hysterically.

"Oh, don't do that, Mrs. Murphy. Hold on, now. Don't do that, my God, let's *talk* about this . . ."

"You try takin' me home, I'll shoot you," said Mom. "I've got a gun in here." She shook her purse violently.

I pulled up with a screech in front of her house. We'd made it in record time, and I had no memory at all of driving it. Mom's arms were folded heavily across her chest and bag; she made no move to leave the car. She didn't budge an inch. I stared at her and knew that short of getting out and hauling her through the passenger door, or opening her door and planting both feet against her and giving her an outward heave, I didn't really see how I *was* to get rid of her. Besides, there was that purse, with or without its hidden gun. I was inclined to think, this time around, she really had come armed.

I screeched the car away from the curb, my eyes hot and dry, my chest bursting with the ballooning inadequacy of my position.

"Mr. Murphy's gonna hear about tonight!" I threatened her hysterically, as if I really thought she cared what her third husband believed.

"I have a *lot* to tell him, *years* of it . . ."

I put my foot to the floor, and sure enough, she started laughing, harsh and uncontrolled.

"Oh, he won't hear a thing from you, you little bitch!

120

You do one thing I don't like, I'll blow your brains all over the street!"

Loretta moaned in agony.

I headed for the only partial sanctuary I'd ever known—Aunt Ruth. Being Mom's older sister and so much bigger besides, she was the only one who'd ever made the slightest effort to pull Mom off me and save my life.

I took the car almost up onto the curb, leaped out before it had even fully stopped, and raced for the front door. Mom came tearing after, but I made it in good time, my robe billowing out behind me as I ran. The door was unlocked—it always was this early, people coming and going, as when I was younger—and I dashed through the entry and up the steps and locked myself in the bathroom.

Long second of silence, then Mom shouting and Aunt Ruth's lower, harsher tones bringing back vivid memories of years ago. They were down by the landing, their voices mixing in a meaningless howl, then fading back, further and further, as if they'd shoved and tossed one another toward the kitchen at the back of the house.

I didn't give myself time to be afraid. It was my graduation night. I couldn't cower by the toilet. I wasn't the child Doris.

Back down the steps then, not stealthy at all, racing, and hearing the steps creak and give me away.

Loretta had finally extricated herself from the back seat of the car. She was in front, the passenger side locked tight, and I leaped into the driver's seat and took off.

And out came my mother, waving her arms over her head. She raced wildly down the walk and out into the street. She grabbed onto the little opening made by my front widow vent, clenching both fists there and howling obscenities in my face.

I was shaking so hard I could barely work the gears, filled

121

with such overwhelming hatred at that moment that Louise Evelyn McMillon had stopped being my mother; she was only an enemy in the street. I meant to run her over; that was my only clear goal. I'd roll this car all over her body if I had to, and toward that end I started down the street. Mom, hanging on, was dragged alongside, running heavily, too winded to keep shouting.

She finally let go. Dropped back. As I screeched the car around the corner, there she still was, in the middle of the street, staring after us.

It seemed I was destined to act in these comedies. No prolonged oases of calm. Inside, I was seething, trapped, and helpless, already the product of all the lessons and traumas of my life.

I couldn't climb out of my depression to try to find perspective or hope. For days after graduation, I locked myself inside myself and shared this latest trial with no one at all. I could have talked to Loretta, or Margaret, or even Dad, but I chose to internalize the misery, hurting like hell. I couldn't ask for help or begin to help myself.

It would have been easier, I could have lived each day just for itself, if Mom hadn't taken to calling. Every evening, over and over. This was much worse than the notes on the car when I lived with Ed Woodman. That was one-sided—I wasn't expected to comment or make a return.

But the phone calls were a continuing ordeal that darkened each night, every single time the phone rang on the desk.

I was genuinely afraid of her. I thought she was totally nuts.

I tried to get up the courage to call and confront Dad. I needed the same basic answers I'd wanted from Grandma. What was Mom like when she was younger, when they were first married? Had she always been irrational and violent? Why hadn't anybody ever gotten her help? Surely, Dad must have seen she wasn't well?

It was a mistake when I finally made the call. It didn't help, and it only made me angry at him.

"She was never what you might call 'right,'" Dad said flatly, safe back in Omaha after that terrible night and our aborted dinner. "She'd always go off, you could never reason with Louise, she got her mind set and she never after let herself see reason.

"She was always," he added—gross understatement—"strange."

I felt a terrible, vast relief. She'd *always* been strange. Then, sharp anger dawned as I saw the full extent to which I'd been victimized.

"Then why didn't you get her professional help? Psychiatric services must have been available to you through the Air Force. . . ."

He hesitated. "I suppose I considered it," he finally admitted. "She'd never have agreed."

"You don't know that," I protested, trying to stay calm. "Maybe she just wanted proof somebody cared enough to take her in hand, to make her do what was good for herself. . . ."

But I couldn't even begin to picture her agreeing to analysis as a solution for her problems.

"I'd never have been free," he said abruptly, his voice still gentle, but I heard the strain in his tone clearly.

"What?"

"I'd never have been able to have a life for myself. They'd have put her away, and though I loved her—I loved her dearly, I did truly, you know that, Doris—I'd have been locked up there with her to all intents, because if she'd been locked away I would never have felt I could divorce her!"

Mom kept calling. And I kept hanging up each time I heard her say "Doris." And the days and weeks passed, and

123

graduation became history. I felt so much more comfortable having no contact at all with Mom, that it was only natural the guilt would start mushrooming. After all, wasn't I leaving her to soak in her mental problems, without making the slightest effort to help?

But I didn't know how to help her. And I was more afraid of her than I cared to admit, even to myself. My physical fear of her violence extended to my belongings, most notably my car, which I'd actually taken to parking in obscure lots rather than openly in front of my apartment. I had endless nightmares throughout that time, seeing Mom creeping through shadows with a hammer or a knife. I'd wake from these dreams knowing very well where they'd started, but the knowledge didn't help; I'd only dream again the next night.

By the end of the second month the fear, guilt, and rage had all merged. I was miserable. It was the most prolonged depression, to date, of my life.

Finally, one evening, one lamp lit in the apartment, down to my last nerve, I answered the ringing phone and didn't hang up.

"Doris . . ."

"I don't want to hear you say anything," I said flatly, trying desperately to keep my voice from going shrill. "*You* listen to me for once. If you ever in your life raise a hand to me again, I will knock you down like any crazy stranger in the street, like any other sick maniac!

"I have nothing else to say to you and there's nothing you could say that I'd be interested in hearing, so stop calling me. You'll never have the chance to embarrass me again!"

I could hear her breathing. I put the phone back on the cradle.

To my amazement, she called again the following night, and all the intervening weeks of guilt and pain and doubt

124

might never have happened, according to the line she followed from that time on.

"My God, Doris," she said as I picked up the phone, "I can't take these prices at the supermarket much longer!"

I stood there and stared, totally blank, at the wall.

"I don't know if you eat much meat, but we're down to chicken and fish. Have you *seen* what they want for pork chops this week . . .?"

She never said another word about the rift in our relationship or about my graduation, or about her behavior or the months that had passed without us speaking. She called every few nights and talked about the cost of living, news headlines, her worries over her own health. She'd grown obsessed with the thought that there was something wrong with her breasts or her head or her legs. She was sure they were cancerous, though her check-ups had been excellent.

I hung up from these calls tired and depressed.

Hearing about health matters set my nerves on edge. It made me wonder, as I'd wondered when I was younger, what I might have inherited from Josefine or from my natural father. What I might carry, unknown to myself, that could be passed on to my children if I ever got married. These thoughts had haunted me for a very long time. The only solution seemed radical: no marriage, no kids, no problem.

It was a path that seemed more logical the older I grew. And I hadn't any real reason to regret my aloneness. It wasn't as if I'd witnessed happiness or security in my parents' relationship.

Nor had I ever felt worthy in myself, as a child must. How could I possibly, when Dad, who'd been the supportive parent, disappeared from my everyday life?

Dad, who'd praised me and listened to me talk about myself. Who'd made a fuss over every little accomplishment and, above all, who'd been fair, even in trying to paint a balancing picture for me of Josefine. Dad had always tried to boost me up, but it was Mom who had me most of my life—all the time after the move to Detroit and the divorce. And it was Mom's valuation, not only of myself but also of Josefine, that stuck hard and fast, twisting everything.

It's obvious now that somewhere along the line I'd determined never again to be vulnerable. I'd refused to let anyone into my life, which meant no one could possibly hurt or disappoint me. My relationships with men were planned to be temporary and safe. I chose situations where no permanency was remotely possible. It left me emotionally free, and also emotionally sterile. It meant I couldn't experience love and also that I couldn't be rejected.

Even then, immersed in the start of a potentially glowing career, I felt a deep, untouchable loneliness I clearly recall today.

My need to find Josefine took a stranglehold again. I thought about the contacts I'd been making ever since I'd gone into communications. I remembered my method of talking my desires around when I'd wanted an "in" to broadcasting. I considered fully, for the first time, that what worked once could work again, this time to find Josefine.

Oh, not right away, of course. Once more, I procrastinated. Not when I had to deal with the mood swings of Louise Evelyn. All I had to remember was her behavior with Lena, and Josefine stayed tucked safe inside my imagination.

But it provided a new twist to the old fantasy. Finding Josefine would allow me to free myself from this emotional deep freeze I found myself trapped in. If I could know the basic truths of my beginnings, the deadly emptiness might ease and I might not be so frightened of showing vulnerability. The fear of all I didn't know, the great mystery of myself, would finally be explained. I might stop being terrified of love. I might be able to make emotional commitments.

It occurred to me that this was one hell of a load to lay on a stranger in Germany. But after all, she owed it all to me. Didn't she?

I could play with these thoughts in the silent dark, and eventually I'd sleep.

One day I was able to tell Margaret about Louise. That this represented a milestone, a reaching out to someone, a willingness, however tenuous, to chance indifference on her part, simply didn't arise between us. It was time to talk to Margaret about things that really mattered. I felt, despite all my natural misgivings, that our friendship was actually special.

"Isn't it possible your mother was overloaded?" she asked, when I told her what had happened at graduation.

"Overloaded?"

"She was carrying around this load of jealousy of Lena, the pain and loss over her own marriage to your dad. She must have seen your sending money for their trip as a very potent kind of treachery on your part. After all, Detroit's *her* town. And from what you tell me, Tom Turner's presence at your planned dinner with your dad and his family had to be the last straw."

"You're saying she had every right to beat me up in front of Cobo Hall?" I asked with interest, staring at her.

She grinned. "No, fool. What I'm saying is, given the portrait you've painted me of your mother, over all the years *before* you ever got near your graduation, it's not hard to understand what motivated her in that particular instance. If she's always been unstable, even at the best of times, when everything seemed to be going her way and nobody could possibly understand why she was flying off the handle, well then, look at it. Your graduation night was just too much for her to bear.

"Which isn't your fault, and shouldn't have been your problem," she added flatly. "But which you should possibly have been able to foresee as a likely thing to happen, anyway."

She was right, of course. But I hadn't wanted to see. I'd blinded myself to it because I so desperately wanted Dad at my graduation.

I looked at Margaret, sitting so easy and relaxed on the couch, her head back against the cushion, her legs curled up under her.

"Until now, I've never been able to really confide in anyone about the ugliness of my relationship with my mother. I don't know why I'm telling *you*. It's not your problem."

"You *should* talk it all out," she said comfortably. "It seems less when the light hits it, like nightmares, doesn't it?"

"I don't like losing self-sufficiency," I said, grimly. "And telling all your problems, to get a sympathy vote, never rated very high with me."

She looked genuinely surprised, sitting up straight.

"Self-sufficient? You're one of the most self-sufficient people I've ever met. That impressed me the first time we met. You had your own place. Your own things. You always had an aura of class. We were both black, we had certain things in common, but with you there were things left out, and other things added. That was interesting," she admitted, smiling, remembering.

"You're my big mystery," she said, grinning.

I thought that was strange, anybody considering me complex enough to make mysteries. It wasn't how I saw myself. I thought I was pretty simple and easy to read.

"You're my runnin' buddy, girl," Margaret said, looking at me. "I'll always be interested to know what you're thinking about. And I'll be here when you need me."

128

NINE

WORK WAS A LOT easier without school on the side. Even so, I still found myself too often working overnight. I'd been establishing contacts in the Detroit police and sheriff's departments, and I'd always been as fair as I could in my reporting, so our relationships were good ones.

Sergeant Fred Williams' voice grew familiar during this time. He was one of the overnight officers in the police department. He was always frank and honest, discussing business, and it was a pleasure to talk to him. I knew I could count on whatever he said, and what he said one day was personal.

NBC was starting a new news service. They were looking for a black woman reporter. Fred had this information from a contact in Cleveland, a correspondent. He passed it along to me with the suggestion that I might want to look into it.

The very prospect of a move like this was mind-boggling. It was a prod, making it impossible to be complacent. It was encouragement, too, a sign that success stories really can happen when the timing's right and you're not afraid to put yourself forward.

But the more I considered it that night, the more nervous the thought made me. After all, I was ridiculously light on experience. Being optimistic was one thing. Actually thinking they'd be interested was quite another matter. It would be a waste of time even to look into it. This kind of job was a plum, which meant thousands of highly qualified women would be vying for it.

Well, maybe not thousands. The requirements were certainly limiting. A black woman reporter. The experience could be assumed. But why assume every black woman reporter with more experience than mine would even be interested in this job in New York?

Of course, all that aside, the bottom line was my feeling that it was crass disloyalty to consider changing jobs now, when JR had invested so much time and energy in teaching me.

I found it impossible those next few days to make up my mind whether or not to apply. I don't know if I ever would have followed it up if nothing else had happened. I don't know if I could have overcome my guilt and self-doubt, even though it was the obvious right direction to take, as right as that secondary school admissions test long ago.

If I'd been waiting for a sign to point me along the way, I didn't have to wait long. A few days after I spoke to Fred, a brochure came to the office. It fully described the new NBC program. Their concept was an all-news format.

My boss, Dave White, thought it was ridiculous. I was absolutely certain it wasn't. I knew, instinctively, that the format would work, and I felt excited by the concept. The thought that I might, just possibly, be part of it was enough to stifle any remaining negative feelings. I sent my brief résumé, a tape, and my picture to the executive producer in New York.

Fred had told me about the program in late March of 1975. In April I got a telephone call to come to New York for an interview.

I hung up from that call, euphoric. I hadn't a single doubt—if I went to be interviewed, I'd land the job. This wasn't even egotism. It was fate, already decided. If! If I took that one more step and actually went to New York.

It was a potentially enormous career move.

I'd only been at WJR for nineteen months. I was still so green it embarrassed me. Maybe I should avoid this whole thing. It wasn't too late. I could change my mind and send my regrets.

Of course, I did no such thing. I'd set myself a hard road to travel, improbable goals to achieve, since I half-believed true success—at least in my mother's terms—was inaccessible. Yet I had to be somebody, and this was quite a place to start.

I looked up plane schedules and prepared myself for my interview.

The executive producer's name was Alan. He had a great deep voice. It made everything he said sound portentous whether it was or not. He kept my interview simple. He said they'd already decided I was what they wanted. Then he turned to the huge chalkboard on the wall behind the desk, picked up a thick piece of unbroken chalk, and wrote a figure:

$43,000

"Go back to your station and give them two weeks' notice and take a week off and be back here on May 15."

He hadn't bothered to ask me *my* opinion of the whole business. Possibly my face said everything for me.

"If they don't like it," he added, calmly, "and try to make things nasty, ask them if they're willing to beat our price."

I didn't know how to tell Dave White I was leaving. I was only twenty-three years old. I hadn't developed a repertoire of bland egotism. In the end, I just blurted out that I had the chance at a great career opportunity. I told Dave I needed to discuss the possibilities with him. That I wanted his opinion.

Of course, what I wanted was his assurance I'd succeed, and along with that, his blessing.

"It's a good offer, Dave. It's a *great* offer. And it *is* New York!"

He grinned. "Come on now, Doris. Don't exaggerate. You've always been a little starstruck. You'd probably think anything with New York City written around it was great, and you know it!"

"Maybe so," I admitted, "but this really is a great offer. I'm not exaggerating," I assured him.

"How great? You're just dying to tell me, aren't you?" I could see he was humoring me.

"Guess," I said, not to be cute, though that's almost certainly what he thought, but only because I was totally incapable of saying such a figure to Dave White. My God, I was making $11,500 at JR. How could I tell him I'd be jumping to $43,000 which was almost surely more than *his* salary? Me, the little colored girl out of Detroit they'd been good enough to take in and train and expect to keep long enough to make it all profitable.

He stirred, growing a little impatient with me.

"I hate guessing games, Doris . . ."

"Guess."

"Eighteen."

132

"More." I felt smug, denying his low estimate.

He sighed. "Twenty."

"More."

That did get his full attention. He stared at me for a second.

"More than twenty?" There was doubt in his tone, and the bantering quality I'd always associated with him was suddenly gone.

I nodded, my smugness evaporating at the chill thought of his actually hitting on the right number.

"Twenty-five." His voice seemed far away, outside the humming in my ears, and I merely shook my head, unable to speak.

Dave waited out a solid ten-count. "Thirty-six," he finally said quite softly. It was a dare.

"Forty-three." I whispered.

He was absolutely silent for an eternity; then he shuffled some papers around on his desk.

"Congratulations." He didn't look at me. "We'll have to throw you a luncheon before you leave."

I was scheduled to leave the first week in May. It seemed like a very short time for goodbyes. I'd grown so close to these people who'd not only given me my first chance in the business, but spared no efforts to train me in all its aspects.

All the other reporters, my friends and teachers at JR, my long-time supports, seemed suddenly strange, almost distant. There was embarrassment now where there'd only been comfortable camaraderie for all the time of my employment. I understood perfectly the mixed emotions they all felt. The desire to be happy for me. The feeling that a lot of steps had been missed in my climb toward this new position.

My last day at WJR rolled around, finally. I'd been miserable in the solitude of my triumph. I felt that old sense of

133

loss, of security gone, all over again. Only this time, *I* was leaving, and I couldn't seem to find the words to draw the others out. It was so much easier just to stay off by myself, already one of the outsiders at the station, no longer belonging with the rest.

"Doris?"

I glanced up from the papers I was shoving into a folder. It was Bill Curnow.

"I want to talk to you, Doris. Come have a cup of coffee."

It was a rainy day—warm and misty. It was spring, and I was about to embark on a huge, scary adventure. I needed my friends to stay my friends and send me off with their blessings. Maybe that was childish, but I really couldn't help it.

"You have to understand, Doris, if we seem less than spontaneous. We're all veterans in this business. We've spent more time clawing our way up to exactly where we stand than you could begin to imagine. Our horizons sometimes seem unbearably limited. Most of us have reached an end goal after all these years of someday being the news director. But Dave doesn't seem to be going anywhere, which means we're all stuck in our current positions. Unless something miraculous opened up for one of us somewhere else— like New York or another really big city—what we're all facing here is a slow and monotonous career death.

"We don't expect you to understand this. You're understandably tied up in yourself and this absolute peach of a chance you've landed. Don't blame us for feeling we've all stood in line a lot longer than you, and that we're all talented enough to deserve the same breaks."

I did understand that. The truth was, I understood it only too clearly. There was quite a large smattering of guilt wrapped around the thrill of landing the job in New York.

"Anyway," Bill said, smiling, "I wanted you to know I

134

am genuinely happy for you. We all are. We really do separate the wish it was each of us going, and the happiness we feel for *your* success!"

Last scene in that closing chapter of my life. The story of my new job hit the local papers:

LOCAL GIRL MAKES GOOD
$43,000 PLUS FRINGES!

It sparked a phone call from Mom.

"Is this true, Doris? About the job in New York?"

I'd already told her about the job, floored by it, when I'd gotten home from New York. I was, therefore, understandably startled by the confusion in her voice. Warning bells, dormant for some time, went off.

"You're taking it?" She sounded breathless and upset.

"Taking it?" My brain went paralyzed at the thought of *not* taking the job. I'd been dreaming of nothing else but New York and my new life. In my head I was already established, getting sophisticated, moving up.

"You're a young girl. It's so much so fast."

I made myself try to understand what she was feeling. I wanted desperately not to sound impatient or annoyed. I felt badly enough about what I couldn't help viewing as my stupendous "good luck." I didn't want "luck" involved. I wanted the clean feeling of totally deserving whatever I gained in life. But I was learning that if you're too damned introspective, you'll never feel you've earned anything you get. Especially if you have to field phone calls full of surprise reactions from Louise Evelyn.

"You've hardly been out of school at all, you're just starting your life and your career," she said numbly.

A short silence, then, while I struggled for something to

say and came up blank, smarting and infuriated by her total lack of enthusiasm or congratulations.

"I'm very happy for you," she said abruptly, then the line went dead.

Happy! Of course, she was happy. She just didn't know how to express her happiness—a condition I should have understood by now. And if Josefine *would* have known how to show pleasure, well, Josefine knew *all* the appropriate reactions. Wasn't that so? Wasn't that the root of my fantasies? Josefine wouldn't have made my whole life hell to begin with.

"Happy." I said it out loud to the empty room, bitterly wondering if Louise could have managed some enthusiasm if she was discussing this same job opportunity with her "own" daughter, Caroline.

I had no real ties here. I didn't belong and I never had. It was time, long past time, I was leaving to start my life.

II

OAKS

TEN

I WAS TWENTY-THREE years old when I got to New York, ready to fall in love with the city and let it fill me up. It fit in so neatly with my dreams about myself. It was the perfect springboard from which to go anywhere I wanted.

Unfortunately, all the hang-ups, the emotional insecurities, the childhood fears and nightmares went with me. . . .

Margaret came to New York to help me set up. She stayed only a week, but it made all the difference. All the "firsts" were natural and easy. Even finding an apartment in a high-rise in Lincoln Center, right in midtown, hideously expensive—even that wasn't out of the ordinary, doing it with Margaret.

The apartment sat right across the street from the WABC studio and started me fantasizing right from the start about someday anchoring the news on television.

While Margaret was with me, I felt lighthearted and free.

139

I was about to make big money. I could afford big things. I might even become famous at the tender age of twenty-three. . . .

But when Margaret was gone, when work was the main event, that's when apprehension took hold and I knew I was out of my depth. I'd never been scared at WJR because I'd been carefully walked through all the routines. In New York, at NBC, I was expected to be a veteran, like the people working alongside me, and I wasn't a veteran. I was only minimally experienced. My self-confidence never *had* been high. It went downhill rapidly.

From May of 1975 until May of 1976, the period of time I worked for NBC, I lived in the constant fear of someone exposing my inexperience. All the other talent had been pulled from prime jobs after long years in the business. Some of my "peers" had worked longer than I'd even lived.

I had WJR for my sole credit. It was ridiculous.

Every day was a new effort just to keep afloat. I knew from day one I was in for it. With that negative attitude, I had to go down. Self-fulfilling prophecies.

Once again, I'd pulled the overnight shift, and the old problems of adjustment were back. I couldn't stay awake, and I certainly couldn't fall asleep. The physical misery added to my emotional insecurity.

I swear I could hear Louise Evelyn in my dreams.

"You should make a place for someone deserving, girl. You never were deserving, Doris. . . ."

But I had to make it work. It was a vital step toward every other goal. I'd wake up at nine in the evening and get to work at ten. I'd write for two hours and go on the air at 12:06. Off at two A.M. Write for two more hours and back on at four. Off at six then and home to try to sleep, and I didn't know if I was coming or going or just cracking up from exhaustion.

I'll never forget my first trip home to Detroit, playing my

"star" role for all it was worth, dressed in jeans and a fur coat. Oh, I was an undeniable hit in Detroit, though, as usual, I didn't know what my mother really thought. And once back in New York, I was floundering again anyway, feeling insignificant in my professional self.

I spent tons of time in introspection. I made some personal tapes, talking through my feelings. I tried to be philosophical and emotionally cool in my monologues on the effects of a brutal childhood. Hadn't Mom outdone herself, stressing all my faults? Convincing me of the irrevocability of "blood always tells"? Taunting me with the elusive facts of my earliest life, then hounding me with endless horrible references to Josefine's lack of morals? Demanding success, then deprecating each upward move for not being nearly successful enough?

These attempts at self-analysis weren't successful. I understand now that the focus was wrong—I was looking backward, reliving old grievances, when I should have been concentrating my thoughts and strength ahead, to new achievements.

It was long past time to come to grips with myself. I had some very big dreams, and here I was, screwing up. I was fettered with a gutter-level lack of self-esteem, and when you don't like yourself, you believe everyone else can run circles around you.

My contract was up in May of 1976. A couple of months before, I decided I'd be smart to try to get some of my eggs in some other basket. My dream was still to be on television, ultimately anchoring the news, but everyone told me there wasn't a hope. You had to leave New York and break in somewhere else if you wanted eventually to come back and try your luck.

I didn't believe that. I couldn't afford to. It was too important to what was left of my self-esteem to find a new job

141

right here, in this city where I knew I belonged, a job with future career potential, where I'd be initially recognized as the novice I was and where I could learn the ropes and stop feeling overwhelmed.

Channel 5, Metromedia, WNEW, was a big independent. It seemed reasonable to try for my start in television with them. They'd been doing some hiring, and I felt I had a chance, though it wasn't an easy decision; I'd had a year of career ego-crushing to pull me down—frosting on the cake after years of Louise Evelyn.

I put on my fur coat to give me some heart and marched myself over to try for an interview with the news director, Mark Monsky.

Monsky was unavailable. His managing editor, John Parsons Peditto—J.P.—agreed to see me, and surprised me considerably.

"I've spent some warm nights with you, Doris," he said, grinning broadly and showing the gap between his two front teeth. His hair stood on end in a bright red shock, and a wave of good humor accompanied his every word and gesture.

"I've listened to you on the News and Information Service, Overnight. I like your style. Frank and warm—unbeatable!"

From somewhere inside myself, observing my own reactions, I was careful not to show what I felt, which was shocked amazement. Maybe I'd actually pictured my lousy self-evaluations etched in New York's concrete. For the first time since arriving in New York, I remembered how natural and right I'd felt when working at WJR. I remembered there actually was good solid rationale for my being in this business. I was capable of excelling. With the right training I could make the job work.

J.P. talked to me for some time. He asked me a lot of

142

questions and listened intently to my answers. He was positive and gave me confidence.

"You're hitting us at a really good time. We're looking for fresh new talent. Says something for your sense of timing, doesn't it?"

But then I'd always known the importance of timing. There'd been whole days and weeks and months and years when that was the rope I'd clung to, telling myself I had it.

J.P. promised to recommend me to his boss.

"By the way," he called after me as I made my way out, "the on-air impression's dead right!"

Two days later, Mark Monsky called. He told me he was impressed by J.P's recommendation. Impressed enough to have decided on a summer competition. Three hopefuls, counting myself, would be battling it out for two positions.

My contract with NBC wasn't to be renewed. I put all my eggs in one basket again, determined to win one of the slots at WNEW.

I spent that summer working twelve and fifteen hours a day. Kevin Hammond, Eddie Thalrose, and Michael Gorman were my first camera crew. They took me out and showed me the ropes, walking me through each step. That's when I knew I'd hit the right slot again. It was the same sense of fitting in that made everything easy at WJR radio.

In at eight in the morning. There, most days, until eleven at night when the news went off the air. The assignment editor would look through all the papers, listen to the radio, check the wire service and the daybook—which lets you know what's going on in the city—and then I'd get my daily assignments. There were mornings I'd arrive as a story was breaking. The crew would already be gone. I'd have to grab a cab or else hunt up a station courier to drive me to the location of the assignment. I learned to live with my tape recorder and my notebook in my pocket, and I'd never felt so totally alive as when I was racing around breathless.

My first stand-up was a piece on tenants' rights. The crew was giving me instructions. Stand here. Look this way. A crowd had gathered. I guess it was obvious how green I was, but I'd written one hell of a closing speech, and I felt good reeling it off. Not a single word botched. Not a blooper in the bunch. I rolled the last sentence triumphantly off my tongue and smiled into the camera.

"For Channel 5 News, this is . . ."

There was the oddest blank inside my head. I stared at the camera eye, then beyond, at the incredulous face of Kevin Hammond.

"This is . . ."

No dice. Numb void. Amnesia. Kevin's face split into a broad grin, and I heard the crowd shifting and whispering.

"Oh, hell . . ."

Laughter, on all sides.

"Can we get the last part over . . . ?"

"Green" doesn't even begin to describe it.

I was on the air from the start, learning so much in such a short time that I never doubted for a minute I'd hook one of the permanent slots.

At the end of my first week on the job, we were on our way back to the station after covering one story when a call came over the radio about a shooting in Harlem.

Around 114th Street, we saw the police barricades. We were allowed to cross police lines, wearing our press badges. A Cadillac was the center of attention on the street. I came up on the passenger side, fumbling with both my tape recorder and my notebook, stooping to look in the front window.

Two black men were in the car. The driver was slumped over the steering wheel, and I couldn't see him properly.

His passenger, closer, only inches away, sat with his head lolling in a broken-doll travesty that was somehow worse than the blood streaking from what was left of his face.

All the street sounds—police radio crackling, kids yelling—backed off behind a persistent hum. It was hot, too; I hadn't known until that moment how hot the day felt. The heat was internal, up through my throat and on into my head. The total image of the inside of that Cadillac made a gray, silent, still shot. I was myself, outside myself, directing my own act. It was a new, strange, anchoring feeling, understanding that the shock would pass because it *had* to pass. That I'd then function normally without showing vulnerability because I could not *ever* be vulnerable if I hoped to succeed in this very cutthroat business. If I thought out every move, didn't let myself just react, I could handle dead bodies or anything else.

Anything or *anybody*. Time to grow up.

I wasn't a scared child cringing by the toilet anymore. I wasn't a young woman suffering from arrested emotional development, smashing up her roommate's car, then puking all over the apartment.

I was a professional, gathering facts, and facts weren't threatening. Fact: These two men in the car were dead. Click. Recorded forever. Their bodies sat like dummies when decency should have had them neatly bagged and put away before we got there, but dummylike they still sat and that fact had to be dealt with. I was embarrassed to keep looking, yet oddly unable to stop; after all, it was why I'd been sent here, to gather all the facts. And after an eternity, someone touched my shoulder, releasing me from blind, face-saving contemplation, and only then did I fully realize I was still standing bent over, gawking at two dead people.

I straightened. I noticed the crowds on the street. I saw, for the first time, the back window of the car, the windshield, too, both shattered, presumably from gunshots. I heard the kids for the first time, clearly, trying to outshout one another for attention, and started thinking slowly and painfully about the best presentation of this story.

"Hey, you. You a TV reporter? Put me on TV, lady. I can tell you everything. I saw it, there was this boy, maybe thirteen years old, on a bike, he come along the street and blew these guys away. . . . This gonna be on tonight? Here. Get a shot of my main man here, with me. . . ."

There was a run on dead body stories that next week. After the first few days, I started having terrible nightmares, seeing them walking and turning into one another, faceless. We covered murder after murder that steaming hot summer, and I kept myself cool and outwardly uninvolved, then moved right on to art fairs and street festivals. And memories of shattered glass and blood and popped eyeballs mixed in my dreams with oil paints and sculpture and lavish gourmet food spreads. . . .

A long step from pretty fantasy dreaming, centering on myself.

I was covering up to three stories a day during the week. Maybe four on the weekend, which meant a lot of hard work. We'd go out and cover the stories, come back to the studio and write them up, then sit in with the editors to explain how each story should be put together for broadcast.

We went down to South Street Seaport one day to cover Operation Sail. The Tall Ships were coming in, and we thought it might be interesting not only to cover the arrival but also the thoughts, patriotic or otherwise, of the people waiting there.

My cameraman on that assignment was Jerry Kahn, and like everyone else at WNEW, he'd never appeared to regard

146

me as temporary or pathetically green, but had always worked in perfect synchronization with my needs.

It was this overall professional acceptance that formed a large part of my instant sense of well-being. I saw my own ultimate success mirrored in the positive attitudes of the people teaching and assisting me.

"Let's get some up-close personal stuff," I suggested. "Then we can finish off with the set shots everybody'll expect, of the ships."

It was early in the day, and even more crowded than I'd expected. Street vendors were setting up, and the endless motion back and forth, the piles of merchandise appearing wherever we tried to walk, the shouted questions, greetings, laughter, and profanity were bedlam, semi-controlled. Even so, shrill and persistent above all the other noise howled one independent, ranting voice. It belonged to one of the vendors, who was stalking around, heaving things not out of but into boxes.

"I'm Doris McMillon, WNEW. Are you coming or going?" I smiled, nodding at the boxed piles.

"Going," he said shortly.

"Better location someplace else?" I heard the disbelief in my own voice. His present site couldn't have been more perfect.

"No," his mouth shut with a snap.

"It's obvious there's a problem," I persisted. "And it seems to have nothing to do with the business potential in this location."

He scowled at me. "Plenty of business if you can afford it," he snarled.

"Excuse me?" First hint there was more here than a single disgruntled man with a narrow personal gripe.

He looked at me, then back behind me at my cameraman and primmed his lips together, glancing to right and left.

147

"I really can't believe *you'd* be afraid of anything," I said, truthfully enough, eyeing his broad shoulders and heavily muscled build. "Especially not on a day like this." I just barely kept myself from looking over my own shoulder for the hordes of other reporters I was sure had to be sniffing out this item with me.

He rubbed his hand over his mouth and eyed me doubtfully. Seemed to balance things in his head, and his grievance won out.

"Okay."

He moved close, his head bent to mine. I knew Jerry's camera was blocked, but that wasn't important for the moment.

"It's not just me." He stuffed his hands in the pockets of battered old chinos. "This won't be the only stand you see the back of today, see? It's these bums, three of 'em—if it was one or even two, you figure, shit, they're just *bums!* See?"

He looked at me and I nodded, though inspiration was only dawning slowly.

"And when they said they were just part of Operation Sail, well, shit! I mean, you *know!* And they *know* you know. See? But what the hell you supposed to do with three of them and your whole life set up and easy to crunch to dust before you can sneeze?"

Jerry was murmuring, trying to maneuver up closer, but the crowds were getting too thick. My vendor friend put up his hand, palm out, warding off publicity.

"I don't want to see my face on the television, lady. And if you're smart, you'll go take pretty pictures of the ships and the river.

"Shit! I don't *have* fifty bucks," he spat, and went back to his vicious repacking.

I moved off a little, and Jerry stepped in my path.

"You gonna go with this?" His voice was resigned. After

all, he knew what reporters were, and he wasn't exactly a still-shot type himself. So we started making the rounds of the vendors. A few wouldn't talk. But most were furious and frightened enough to be voluble—the three-man team had hit on them all. One of the vendors was more than happy to finger this trio for us.

I didn't really think about being cautious or smart. In truth, I felt invulnerable that morning, with Jerry behind me and the crowds all around. It was my first taste of power, and I ran with it. No courage involved. No sense either, just the smell of a story and not another reporter on to it.

I positioned myself just off the main drag and watched the approach of the trio with anticipation. When they were only a couple yards off, I stepped forward and raised my voice.

"I understand you've been out hustling the vendors." I made this flat statement loudly enough to draw interested stares from the passing crowd. A few people hesitated, then stopped, listening. Excellent. I couldn't have asked for more.

Behind me, Jerry's camera was rolling, getting nice tight shots of their faces. The biggest of the three looked me up and down slowly, then turned to his friends and laughed, then pointed a stubby finger at Jerry.

"Get that camera out of my face, freak, or you'll be eating the pieces."

He spit then, a nice glob on the toe of my shoe, sucked on his cigarette and blew smoke straight into my face. Jerry kept filming. I smiled coldly through the smoke, still reassured by the watching crowds, thickening around us now, and by some vague idea that I was protected by my sex and my profession.

After all, who'd be suicidal enough to beat up a woman reporter on-camera, with all those witnesses?

"How many of the vendors have paid you protection?" I persisted, cocooned by this unreasonable, naive sense of security.

The man stared again, aggressively, at Jerry, and tried to step around me, and I sidestepped with him, still blocking him, no doubt aggravating him to distraction. People have flipped out for lots less. I didn't think of that.

He stopped. His shoulders hunched. He looked at me, eyes small and mean and glaring.

"Is it always fifty dollars you demand, or do you just sort of make up the numbers according to how you feel? What's your take so far today?"

His hands twitched and balled, but before I could even think about retreat, one of his friends had pulled him back a step. There was an angry, muttered argument; then all three men turned and elbowed their way through the rapt audience to vanish in the crowds.

I was hot with pleasure all the way back to the station, although Jerry sat silent, hugging his camera. Oddly enough, it was only when we were back on our own safe turf that reaction finally hit me, and I looked more realistically at the whole situation.

I gave some thought to personal safety. And I also remembered the surge of power I'd felt pursuing the story. I weighed these things as honestly as I could and still came up "no contest." It was right for the story to come first, and since it had come out well, it was relatively easy to justify taking chances.

We ran the story that night on the news. The next day I was off. I didn't find out until later that the police viewed our broadcast. That undercover officers set up the next morning as legitimate vendors down at South Street Seaport. Sure enough, back came my friends, the three not-too-bright toughs. The police made their arrest; the station tried to reach me to do a follow-up; and when they couldn't locate me, another reporter at the station, Steve Bauman, went on the air and finished my story up.

But I'd shown myself to have a nose for news and a fair smattering of guts. The station was happy—after all, they had an exclusive—and at the end of that summer, I won my slot.

I became the utility player at WNEW.

I was really too busy now for fantasies. But I did wonder, just in passing, what Josefine would think of her daughter, the television news correspondent.

I did whatever needed doing at WNEW. And because I seemed to thrive on these crazy demands, it was satisfying. And the news being what it is, and reporters being what they are, it was inevitable that one day I'd get to play a role bordering on the melodramatic.

I went undercover to help try to expose a welfare rip-off.

"Now, what we've got here is a tip on a purported welfare fraud. We've got a guy set up at the 135th Street welfare center who's calling himself—get this—an 'income specialist.'"

We were all there—administrative types on down in the news department. None of us needed a rating on this story. If we found the information was essentially correct, if we could manage to get inside the system and expose whatever fraud was taking place, it could even be good enough for Emmy consideration. But that was taking the story last things first.

"This 'income specialist' allegedly watches the applicants come through, sees them fill out all the paperwork, listens in on their answers to the oral questions, then takes some of them aside and says that for a mere two hundred–dollar fee, he'll get them special consideration. Which apparently means a blind eye to any inconsistencies in their statements,

151

and a push to speed up the whole normally time-consuming process.

"Now, what he really does for these people, as we understand it, is nothing. Nothing, that is, but collect his fee. He apparently has a good eye for the applicants who would make the rolls anyway. Whether he actually pulls strings to get unqualified applicants on the welfare rolls is something else again. Of course, we'll find out everything we can.

"But as far as our current information goes, our friend, who calls himself 'Joe,' does nothing at all except make himself rich off the misfortune of these people.

"I want Roggerio and McMillon undercover on this one."

My pencil made a hard little dot and pressed down on the notepad, absolutely still. When I looked up, it was straight across the table into Graciella Roggerio's eyes. She grinned slightly and winked.

"Nobody's likely to recognize you, Roggerio. Associate producers are as anonymous as writers. But you're on the air, McMillon, so come up with a new look. Nothing weird or really different, just a shift in the emphasis, away from tone and on down to 'street.'"

Well, I went into the assignment with a classic approach-avoidance dilemma. First and foremost, I was sure that somebody would recognize me and I'd blow the whole bit. Or that the lies I'd have to tell just wouldn't be convincing. Or that I'd do something so phenomenally stupid I'd jeopardize the total operation.

On the other hand, it was a great opportunity to live a role. My first grown-up acting job—I spent some time deciding on my new "look." I pictured welfare applicants as either bowed-down or brassy-cool, and since bowed-down wouldn't do a thing for my fearful side, I layered brassy-cool all over myself.

I wore a stone-black wig, meant to look phony, huge,

152

gaudy earrings outdazzling my lipstick, skintight jeans, and a flashy polyester shirt; then I stuffed my mouth with gum and commenced popping it continuously.

I'd finally gone ethnic, or at least as ethnic as I'd ever managed to get trying to fit in on the streets of Detroit and having miserably little success.

The questions they asked at the center were endless. There was nothing easy about applying for welfare—not if the paperwork was representative.

I had my story all ready. My common-law husband had left me, and I'd been living with a friend, but my money had run out. I explained that the people who owned the building were threatening to evict me—I even had a pho-nied-up lease for proof I'd been living with somebody and splitting the rent until my luck had gone sour.

"So how *are* you living?" The worker's voice was flat, professing detachment, but I doubted the question was actually on the sheet she was filling out. She raised her eyes as she asked me, then dropped them again, fingers smoothing the edge of the paper, the lines of her face tired and depressed.

I opened my eyes very wide. "Do I *have* to tell you that?"

She looked back at me for a second, then scribbled something on the form, and I craned my neck, trying to see if she'd actually written down "prostitute."

"I had to sell some of my jewelry," I drawled.

Her eyes touched the hideous costume jewelry on my fingers; she chewed at her lip and said nothing.

"I have some men friends," I added, rolling my eyes and touching my hair. "They been helpin' me out."

Scratch, scratch of the pen on the sheet. More questions, a whole list.

That was Phase One. Phase Two was another interview, this one to learn my qualifications in the job market. Phase

Two was dead easy. A general rating of "no talent" leaves little room to maneuver.

"No. I can't type."

"File?"

"'Fraid not."

"Have you ever worked in any job, in any capacity?"

I smiled slightly, lolling in my seat, silent.

"Do you have any skills at all. Skills," the worker amended, "that I can note down?"

"Honey," I said, "I am absolutely without skill. I can't do *nothin'*."

The "income specialist" we were after—Joe—picked up on me that first day at the center. He ogled my tight jeans and my loud blouse, then spent some time in seemingly pointless conversation, making his own assessments while I grinned and chewed and sweat bullets. It didn't help when, suddenly, without preamble, he offered me a pinch from his own private stash, which is how I found myself, seconds later, closeted in the very dim and dirty bathroom at the center.

I stared down at my own hand, clutching a twist of tin foil filled with white powder I took to be cocaine, telling myself it couldn't possibly be real because what kind of half-wit would jeopardize himself like that with a perfect stranger? The only answer I could come up with was I really *looked* my part. That the act I was putting on was eminently successful. It wasn't a flattering thought. But if all that was true, and this really was cocaine, what was I to do with it, and after, how was I to act?

Finally, repulsed by the shaking of my hands, aware I'd been in the bathroom too long and propelled by the fear that that very fact would give me away, I threw a medium pinch of the powder in the toilet, retwisted the foil, exited the ladies' room and handed the foil back to Joe, who was waiting right outside the door.

154

"Thanks a lot," I muttered. "Thanks a lot," I said again, then nodded, then nodded again, then once more for good measure, and grinned broadly at him, licking my lips and laughing—the laughter was pure nerves, but it seemed to sit right. He took back his little present, eyed me up and down, and linked my arm in his, telling me he could get me onto welfare sure and fast for the right price. He hinted he could get me other things, too, if I was interested, then he leered, sweating profusely, while I stared fascinated at his huge, meaty hands and clung to the fiction that I was perfectly safe.

Well, I called Joe two days later. I hadn't been able to get the image of him out of my head. He was a melodramatically sinister-looking man, with a shiny bald head and over-large cold green eyes and a moustache accentuating a mean mouth. And those hands. I could weave whole hideous fantasies around those thick hands.

Joe told me to meet him on a park bench across from the center, at 135th and Broadway. That's where I paid him the money, while the WNEW crew sat in an unmarked van, out on the street, shooting the whole transaction through a hole in the window. Since I was wired, we had every damning word down, too, and every leering innuendo.

Even then, the ordeal wasn't over. We'd informed the police early on of our efforts and kept them updated on our progress, and now it was time to get a policewoman into the system.

By this time, all I wanted was to get myself out. My feelings about what I was doing were mixed—a friend I'd told had come down on me hard. She felt I was treacherous, depriving my own people of money they needed to survive. And while I didn't really believe this, while I was simply determined to right some basic wrongs that tended to deprive the most needy of what they truly deserved, I was frightened enough by Joe and the aura of careless indifference to the law that surrounded his every gesture and word for the guilt feelings to assume larger proportions than they might otherwise have done.

Bottom line was I was looking for an out. My bad feelings were growing. I was afraid of this assignment. Common sense had finally caught up with bravado. But there was one more chore I had to perform. I had to call Joe and tell him I had a friend who was willing to pay him, as I had, to get quickly on welfare.

I wasn't prepared for Joe to agree so quickly. He told me to come right over to his apartment and have my friend meet me. I just barely had time to call the black policewoman, Kathy, but no time to get myself properly wired up for the meeting.

I threw on the tape recorder, taping it to my upper leg, under my pants. There wasn't time to get the wires on under my blouse, so we hooked them out over it, and I buttoned a long leather coat over everything. We raced out to the van, yanked open the door, and the door fell off in the street at my feet.

I had a very bad feeling about this meeting.

Well, Kathy got caught in traffic, which meant I was alone with Joe for forty-five minutes, trying to make puerile conversation and all the while desperately aware of those wires, just hanging there. It was a mildly chilly day, and I started to sweat, and to make matters worse, Joe asked if I was cold and turned the apartment heating up.

I sat there dying, waiting for Kathy to show, while Joe regaled me with a story about dead bodies his friends had carried out of the apartment only days before—solution, he said grinning thinly, to some internal problem.

All the nerves in my body started screeching out warnings. By the time Kathy showed up, I was numb with my own groundless imaginings. Listening to Joe talk, I was sure he knew exactly what game I was playing. That he'd invited

156

me up here for his own sadistic pleasure. That I was about to die. Then he'd call up his friends for another "internal problem body removal."

I couldn't believe my luck when Kathy finally turned up. It was overwhelming anticlimax to be easily dismissed by Joe—he wanted to "interview" Kathy alone. The visual images I'd entertained for the past forty-five minutes were too real and immediate to dismiss easily: I'd actually imagined I felt Joe's hands closing around my neck and choking me to death.

But there I was, outside the closed apartment door, hearing Joe's voice say something suggestive, and then hearing Kathy's throaty laugh. Then I was out on the street, walking fast. It was much too soon to understand that I was free of this business.

Kathy successfully entered the system and paid her two hundred dollars. She made her arrest—it all happened pretty quickly, and we went on the air with the whole story. It was only later that we heard how Joe went berserk. How he promised he'd be back, and when he was, he'd be looking for the lady who'd helped set him up.

Of course he knew my name. There I was on television.

The station, thrilled by our success, put the story in for Emmy consideration. And it did win the Emmy. After all, it was Emmy material. I was so busy by that time, doing every job imaginable. After a while, I lost track of my own frantic schedule. I did sports. I did talk shows. I was forming good working relationships.

I had a two-year contract, and I was running smooth, no more gross horrors of insecurity. New York loved me, and I loved New York, and it didn't even matter much anymore whether I impressed Louise Evelyn or not.

In 1978, Mark Monsky called me in to tell me he wasn't

157

renewing my contract. I was never really sure why I'd been let go, but not long after the station hired a Hispanic.

Mom had never told me she was proud of my achievements, and now that I had time to think, I grew morbid wondering about that. She'd never said I'd met whatever standard she'd set or that she was glad I was her daughter.

It was the pattern of my life. I'd never been good enough at anything I'd tried. Not in winning the scholarship to Concord, or graduating from Cushing, or being accepted to college, or getting my degree. Not in managing the career moves that had taken me through WJR and NBC and on to my television work at WNEW.

I still feel today what I felt so strongly then—that my mother should have been my friend. She should have been someone whose opinion I valued and whose judgment I could trust. Other mothers and daughters reached this point of genuine liking and mutual respect.

My mother should have been there in my times of bursting success. She should have been there, too, when I felt cut loose and barren, not knowing how things could come right again.

I was wrapped up in myself. I didn't want to have to hurt for Louise. I didn't dare imagine what she'd lost through the years. It was easier, by far, to escape to Josefine.

Josefine would have understood. Josefine would *be* like me in her sensitivity and needs. Josefine had feelings and frailties like mine. She'd recognize those traits in her daughter because she'd empathize.

Josefine would ask me the intimate questions that Mom chose to ignore. How I spent my solitary time? What I felt for New York? If I was lonely, despite the people-oriented nature of my work?

She'd ask about my love affairs and why I hadn't settled down.

158

Mom, of course, never asked me any questions, and I concluded she simply didn't care.

But it was Mom who'd taught me to reach for the top. She'd clearly expected that much of me, and I'd learned to expect it of myself. So I had to believe that a door would open to put me back on the air. And I made myself a promise. As soon as my next career move was apparent, I'd really try to find Josefine. I didn't like myself at all for my years of procrastination.

I talked to Margaret long-distance a lot. I also talked to another friend from Detroit—Toni Jones, who now lived in New York.

Toni and I had dinner out one night. Then we came back to my apartment and sat talking about our families, and for the first time, I told her my fantasy about finding Josefine.

"Why wait?" she asked, when I expressed my decision to start searching when I was back in television again.

"I need to get back on top first," I said flatly. "You know, ego strokes. But when I do, no more waiting; I will start talking it around about wanting to find somebody with contacts in Germany."

She was silent for a long time, then finally met my eyes.

"And what about your Mom? Louise? Out in Detroit?"

I had no answer, of course.

"Isn't she the excuse you've always given yourself?" Toni asked. "How badly she'd be hurt? How angry she'd get?"

"I can't worry about that all my life."

"No," she agreed. "But you are worrying about it. It's a huge part of you that you don't even see. You *care* about people, not just your mother and what she'll think or feel. You bleed for the whole world, Doris, and it drains you, and it's probably one of the reasons you put things off— you don't like precipitating problems for anybody."

"I just don't like to see people hurt," I retorted. "Don't make me sound like some wet-spirited marshmallow who

159

bleeds all over everybody regardless of their problem. And of course I wouldn't want to hurt Louise, but I wouldn't want to hurt Josefine either. After all, they're both important to me."

"Great," Toni said. "Now you'll convince yourself you've got Josefine's feelings to deal with, too, if you start this search. And if you let it get you, *that* thought will be your new excuse to just sit back and do nothing. Look how good you'll end up feeling if you leave things like they are—you won't be hurting anybody. Not Louise. Not Josefine."

I gripped my hands together in my lap and said nothing.

Toni leaned toward me, her eyes grave. "Only yourself. That's the only person you don't mind hurting. Don't you think it's long past time you stopped worrying over what Louise's reactions will be and started rounding out your own life?"

I laughed shortly. "My life is well-rounded."

She snorted. "Right! You live solely for your work. You tell me honestly that you give any of the guys you date half a chance? You stay emotionally uninvolved. Well, we're all afraid of something, aren't we?"

She was right, of course, about my relations with men. If I opened myself up, I could find myself emptied out before I was even fully aware what had happened to me.

And of course I feared rejection. That was understandable, wasn't it? In all honesty, after a young life spent around my Mom, I didn't feel I could bear one more rejection. In the total consideration of things, how many women are thrown away by *two* mothers, no reasons given?

It was absurd to think of love, of marriage and children. I hadn't yet found whatever flaw in myself had made me so undeserving.

But if I found Josefine, I'd know it all. There'd be no more secrets.

160

* * *

In the early fall of 1978, Metromedia put on a new program called "Broadway Extra," with Wendy Sherman and
Stuart Klein co-hosting. Doris Bergman, a producer at
WNEW, suggested to Art Star, the executive producer of
"Broadway Extra," that I'd be good freelancing some of the
reports, visiting hotspots around town and highlighting
coming events.

Well, I came back to Metromedia at one hundred dollars a
spot, after six months of odd jobs and oddly restful nights. I
looked and felt terrific, and because I was cool and calm, I
did every story effortlessly. Some great pressure had eased
off. I was back on a high note; everything I touched went
right. And though "Broadway Extra" folded, I'd proven
my value as a freelancer. When the newspaper strike a few
months later resulted in a hungering for news updates,
Mark Monsky called me in and asked me to do one-minute
briefs.

That led to other things over the following months. I
found out that freelancing wasn't a terror-trip in insecurity
but a real independence, a total lack of restriction. When I
was under contract, they'd worked me to death for my set
salary. As a freelancer, I got paid for each single thing I did
and I was the one who decided.

It grew easy, in this environment, to find my ego alive
and thriving. I was full of myself for the first time since I'd
come to New York. I *could* succeed at anything if I believed
it hard enough. Anything! Even initiating my search for
Josefine if I truly desired it. Even that was surely possible if
I was willing to talk my story around. If I could overcome
the endless fear of Louise finding out.

After all, I had promised myself.

Tentatively at first, then with more and more confidence,
I started telling acquaintances my story and asking if they

161

had any contacts in Germany who might be willing and able to help me.

During this same period, I was busier than I'd ever been in my life. I started doing the half-hour Saturday night "Black News." I was filling in as an anchor when needed, and on "Sunday Night Extra," as well. I didn't have much time to worry over the initial lack of response to my story about Josefine. I hadn't expected quick results. I knew I'd be enormously lucky to find one single person with the desire and the ability to help.

Also during this turbulent period, my weather reporting career had its shaky start.

"But I know absolutely, positively nothing about reporting the weather," I protested to Mark when he called me to his office, eleventh-hour style.

"Bob Harris is sick," he barked. "There's nobody else. What the hell difference does it make if you've never done it before? You can think on your feet. You've proven that over and over again. And we need you, so you'll *do* it. You *can* do it! What else do you need to know?"

He grinned then, but it didn't make him look any less determined.

"Go on down, take a look at my beautiful map. Tell yourself how good you'll be. . . ." He was verbally pushing me out the door.

I took myself down, resigned, to the studio. As I'd feared, the weather map showed no state boundaries, yet I was supposed to refer to specific areas in my report. I stared at it thoughtfully. After a minute, I went back up to my desk. When I returned to the studio, it was to lightly pencil in the state names on the map so that only I could see them.

The broadcast went off without a flaw. Afterward, Mark immediately requested my presence in his office. I patted myself on the back all the way there, so pleased at the ease of my latest triumph.

162

Mark was hunched over his desk, blood vessels bunched in his face.

"I just love the way you did the weather," he said, hissing through his teeth. "Now maybe you'll tell me why you fucked up my map? My beautiful fuckin' map! A thousand dollars we spent and you wrote all over it and they CAN'T—GET—OFF—THAT—CRAP!

"Get down there, McMillon. And scrub. Scrub scrub scrub . . . !"

Well, the crew had been scrubbing without any noticeable success, or more accurately, they'd been dabbing at my writing, gently. Of course they weren't getting anyplace. I borrowed some Ajax and a rag from maintenance, and the others stood around, then, watching and grinning. I was amazed how easily the map came clean, and it was only when I stood back, finished, that I saw I'd removed the soft gloss along with all the state names.

Mark's map was never the same again. I think he kept me on doing weekend weather as a penance.

ELEVEN

I MET WILHELM SHUSTER on a Tuesday afternoon at a famous hotel in midtown New York, late November of 1978. I was talking lethargically with two friends—Shirley Brown and Connie Collins—it was my "lady time," my day off from WNEW TV. There was no reason to suspect the day would bring me special gifts. I was gripped with that exhaustion that hits when the immediate need to perform takes a rest. No red-letter omens marked my horizons. And I never expected my first response on the matter of Josefine to finally appear through the upright person of the hotel's maitre d'.

He approached our table and bent low, embarrassed, to whisper to me.

"I beg your pardon, Miss McMillon, but you mentioned your interest in locating someone with good connections in Munich? Well, there's a gentleman over in the corner; his name is Mr. Wilhelm Shuster. I told him your story. He's interested in helping you. He would like you to join him at your convenience.

"Under ordinary circumstances we never involve ourselves in the private affairs of our guests, but he is a long-term patron of the hotel and you *have* spoken to me of your interest. . . ."

I expected everything and nothing as I excused myself from my friends. Lethargy was charged so suddenly with hope and fear that I walked too stiffly, smiled unnaturally as I approached Mr. Shuster's small table.

My first impression, through this odd, dull panic, was of a stereotypical German. I don't know what Wilhelm thought of me as he ordered me a cocktail. But he didn't mind staring openly and cooly as I tried to pretend I wasn't studying *him*.

"You will forgive my intrusion on your private time," he stated flatly. "I have heard you have a mystery to explore, and I've always interested myself in human puzzles like this.

"It is also my understanding that your progress in this matter has, to date, been difficult at best. . . ."

He waited for me to affirm or deny this.

"My progress," I said, trying to match his daunting cool, "has been uninspiring. Zip. Nil."

He smiled slightly, remote twitching of the lips.

"It is my understanding that your reason for—how shall I say?—*broadcasting* your dilemma is so that anyone with German connections might intercede . . . ?"

He spoke so softly I had to lean toward him to hear, which didn't do much for a pose of worldly distance. It seemed best to be flatly truthful, no embellishments.

"I'm just beginning my search, and I couldn't think of a more obvious or easier way than by telling my story to as many people as possible in the hope of finding someone willing to assist me."

He seemed to analyze this fact, still watching me, unblinking. I was hotly uncomfortable and unexpectedly aware that the subject matter of this little chat was very personal to me. Not that his questions involved intimacies. There *were* no intimacies.

"I am an important man in Germany," he stated baldly.

There was more than a glimmer of complacency in his tone, but at best, such a statement would be difficult to make with modesty, and Wilhelm didn't appear particularly modest anyway.

He confirmed this impression immediately.

"I have, I may tell you, special business interests abroad. Not," he stroked his chin, "only in my own country, you understand."

He eyed me, perhaps to see if I was suitably impressed. Actually, I was. I wasn't sure why; the conversation could just as easily have slipped over into farce, but it didn't.

"I also have connections in the secret police," he said portentously.

I just gaped at him.

"I think there would be no problem helping you in your search, if you wish."

Of course I wished. I'd had questions inside my own head for years, but I'd doggedly dismissed them when I'd started talking the story around and asking for assistance. Why, then, this sudden feeling I was being stripped naked? And how could it possibly matter how inexplicably vulnerable talking to this man made me? I couldn't turn down an offer I'd basically solicited. How could I even consider retreat? What the hell was I thinking?

Wilhelm accompanied me back to my table to meet my friends, and when Connie left early, Wilhelm asked both Shirley and me to join him for dinner that evening. We agreed—we were both curious about Wilhelm. We met at J.B. Tipton's Restaurant on the East Side, and he came bearing unexpected gifts—a huge Hermes pink and white scarf

166

for me, Caleche perfume for Shirley. He'd also brought a camera and took endless snapshots, talking all the while, asking questions about my work, the people I knew, my interests, and finally, Josefine.

The evening left me with that same sense of unease I'd felt on being introduced to Wilhelm. He'd given nothing away about his own private self, and so whatever I'd hoped to perceive over dinner that night hadn't materialized, yet I had the feeling Wilhelm *had* learned more than I'd wanted to divulge about *me*.

My imagination was running wild. Nothing new—I always had indulged in idle fantasizing. I didn't know why so great a part of my life should already have been spent romanticizing. But this search was real; whatever we'd find at the end would put a final stop to idle dreaming.

Wilhelm returned to Germany at the end of that week, sending me a note he'd scribbled at the airport:

My Very Dear Doris,

So nice to meet you. I will be in touch.

Wilhelm

The note was folded around a brand-new hundred-dollar bill and an assayer's card attached to a gold ingot, credit Swiss.

I thought of immortalizing Wilhelm on tape, a nice input on my road toward self-discovery, but I decided that I didn't need the emotional workout. I wasn't sure I even believed in Wilhelm.

I'd been trying to sort out my life for some time. I hadn't been very successful at what amounted to talking to myself. It had occurred to me that as a reporter, I should either

167

write down or tape what I felt about my childhood and my relationship with my mother and thereby work it all out. I'd made that resolution more times than I could count, but I'd rarely actually spoken my vulnerability out loud, not even to myself. It could have been a catharsis for childhood nightmares and clinging adult outcomes, if I hadn't been so singularly lousy at interviewing the real Doris McMillon.

Thinking about Wilhelm was part of all that. It was worse after receiving his note, like trying to pinpoint the germs of truth in a fiction. I hadn't liked him very much, but I did want to believe him. I wanted to believe that he liked solving puzzles and that he'd solve the puzzle of Josefine.

A few days after receiving the note, I called Margaret back in Detroit. I needed someone I trusted to play devil's advocate.

"You actually believe this *Wilhelm*'s gonna help you out?" She was really curious.

"Why shouldn't he?" I fell back on the old childhood litany. Believe only the best and only the best could happen to me.

"Why the hell *should* he?" Margaret asked reasonably. "Or didn't that cross your mind? A perfect stranger comes up to you in the middle of a hotel. . . ."

"He asked the maitre d', who's an institution in himself at the hotel, to show me over to his table, which isn't 'just coming up to me. . . .'"

"And propositions you . . ."

"Oooh," I grinned, trying to play it for laughs. "So that's what he wanted. You'll have to admit, it's a novel approach. You think he goes to this much trouble every time he has visions of brown sugarplums . . . ?"

"That's right," Margaret said, "Play the fool. . . ."

But I didn't have the heart for games. I'd been replaying

168

that meeting over and over in my head. I felt jumpy about Wilhelm, or maybe just about Josefine—I couldn't now separate them. And the actual content of our ten-minute talk before we joined Shirley and Connie back at my table was meager to say the least.

His back had been to the window. The chill gray light was *his* instrument for playing *me*.

"Birthplace?" His hands were flat, wide, and very pale, and lay loosely linked on the table. Calm and still, close to his glass which was one-third filled with something yellow-amber. "Munich you *know* or only think?"

"I *know* my father was stationed in Munich."

"Your father . . . This is your father, Horace McMillon?"

His smile sat tight underneath a stare so narrow that the cold blue of his eyes all but vanished in his eyelids.

"Yes. Horace. Mac. Horace McMillon."

"This Josefine Reiser, she would be . . ." he cocked his head, ". . . perhaps fifty? Perhaps younger, considering," a faint twitching of his lips, "considering the circumstances?"

I shrugged. "Maybe. I don't know."

"Odd of your father, wouldn't you agree, telling you this one thing? Not enough to make it easy to find your natural mother and yet much much more than he should have said at all if he did, indeed, desire secrecy?"

For I'd let him think Dad gave me the entire name. It was easier than trying to explain Louise.

"It wasn't odd at the time," I protested. "In the context of the situation, it was natural enough. Besides," I could almost see Dad's expression on that awful afternoon, when I was thirteen, "he knew how much I needed to have something, however small, to hang on to at that moment. There were personal problems. . . ." But I left it at that. It wasn't part of this business. It was none of Wilhelm's concern, or anyone else's.

He'd eyed me coolly, then something in his manner

169

shifted and I felt I was being dismissed—it was as blatant as a goodbye kiss. So strong was the impression that I responded too quickly, hurrying to rise though I hadn't had time to ask *him* anything. He watched me reach for my bag, he himself slow in rising, and I felt a passing sensation then of days long gone, of schoolgirl gaucherie, of knowing I was outclassed without understanding the causes. It was very unsettling.

More so when he'd suddenly decided to accompany me back to my table. He became expansive and pleasant without really warming. And I couldn't shake the feeling that Wilhelm Shuster, for whatever reason, was having a silent little laugh on me.

The last thing he'd said when he'd left Shirley and me after dinner that night should have been reassuring. It should have convinced me he *hadn't* just wanted a date with two black women he'd hooked up with.

"I will be back in Germany at the end of the week. I will keep you informed, if I may, by phone or through the mail, of any possible leads. And you, my very dear Doris," that tight smile again, "really must try to recall anything, however small, that you may have been told about this woman."

"Well," Margaret was saying into my ear, "*did* you remember anything to tell him about Josefine?"

"There's nothing to remember. You know that. I was never *told* anything."

"But if you did remember something, you'd run right out and spill it all to this perfect stranger," she said, certainty ringing clear.

"He's not a perfect stranger. . . ."

"You only just met him, girl. What *does* that make him?"

". . . to the *hotel* or to the maitre d' . . ." I persisted.

"Oh. Now that makes all the difference in the world, doesn't it?"

170

"He's very rich and influential." I sounded stuffy even to myself. "He has a thriving business and he's been a patron of the hotel for the past twenty years. All of which gives him, it seems to me, some claim to respectability."

"You are very young for your age, Doris," Margaret pronounced flatly and with obvious regret, then ruined it with the lighthearted laugh that made it impossible to get aggravated.

But I *was* aggravated. I needed to work it out for myself. I needed to understand my own feelings about Wilhelm, about finding Josefine, and, I suppose, about everything else surrounding my relationship with Louise all my life.

Not a small quest.

"What's your problem anyway?" I asked Margaret. "You didn't hassle me when I told you I was trying this approach. Did you just feel it was safe and a nice little pacifier as long as it didn't produce results?"

Margaret sighed. I could almost see her running her hand slowly through her hair, her head shoved back into the cushion of her favorite chair.

"I just think you shouldn't pin your hopes on somebody who tells you stories about his 'influence' with the 'secret police.'" She burst out laughing, then. "Oh, hell, I'm sorry, girl. It's just so ridiculous. It's got all the makings of a really awful movie, doesn't it?"

Of course it did. And I felt better talking to Margaret, but my call, regarded honestly, hadn't proved a thing. I'd graduated on my own from my first thumping excitement to a filtered-down anticipation that flaked off finally into unexpected apprehension.

What did I really want from Munich? How much could I handle?

Bottom line: What if Wilhelm did find Josefine?

Well, Wilhelm was true to his word. He started sending me letters and occasionally telephoning.

171

December 13, 1978

Dear Doris

We have called 384 Reisers so far, but without success. The search is going with full steam and we try to track down everybody. It is a job for a watchmaker.

Hoping that you are well and looking forward to hear from you, I remain

With best regards,

Sincerely,

Wilhelm

_____

December 18, 1978

Dear Doris,

It is more than looking for a needle in a haystack. Some of the official registration offices keep the files only for ten years, so we are looking for all the Reisers. There are 17 registration offices in Munich and it could have been any hospital in Munich.

Since last week I have also a good friend of the police forces included in the search. Everything is registered under the mother's birthdate. The regional offices keep records also of unmarried women.

Please be sure that I am doing my very best.

Wilhelm

_____

December 29, 1978

Dear Doris,

After our telephone conversation the research was interrupted due to the holidays. Now everything continues almost from the beginning.

172

I have found the birthdate of your mother. Still, it is a tremendous research job. I am hopeful, however, that I will locate her in the near future. People of mine are sneaking around town trying to find friends who might have some answers.

Be assured that I am personally very engaged in this project and keep after it. On the 21st of January I have to leave for the States again to continue some other business in Washington, from where I will call you immediately and see that we get together.

Wishing you all the best for the new year,
I remain,

Sincerely,

Wilhelm

January 11, 1979

Dear Doris,

The search is still going on. We have been concentrating on all kinds of ways and I hope I have some answers some time next week.

Next Sunday I will fly to Washington and as soon as I arrive there I will give you a call.

You know, sometimes during the search I reached a point where I thought I had to give up, because it is such a difficult task. People who were working with me gave up, and I had to replace them.

More details when I see you.
Sincerely yours,

Love,

Wilhelm

Wilhelm flew in and I met him for dinner. He told me all about the search he was conducting—pretty much a rehash of his letters. He seemed vague and distracted when I asked him to elaborate, but I judged I didn't know him well enough to evaluate his manner. Perhaps he was overly cautious by nature. He obviously wanted solid facts before he told me anything more than he'd hinted at already.

He did tell me he thought he might have located Josefine's mother. That one of his people had been trying to get in touch with her and had been, so far, unsuccessful.

Josefine's mother. My grandmother.

"It is becoming expensive," Wilhelm mused, cradling his wine glass and eyeing me over the rim. "But don't worry," he added smoothly. "I'm pleased to be doing this for you."

I was beginning to feel even less happy about this entire arrangement. I was absolutely certain that while no actual "payment" for services had ever been suggested in so many words, I'd be a fool to consider Wilhelm a philanthropist. I'd be better off telling him I'd changed my mind and no longer desired his assistance. But how could I do so when he'd put out so much and when he really hadn't done a thing to turn me off?

Besides, it was obvious he was getting closer and closer to Josefine. I'd have to stick it out and handle "payments" if and when they came up.

Wilhelm made constant business trips throughout the remainder of 1979 and came to see me or take me out for the evening while reporting his latest progress. Unfortunately, the early optimism of his search quickly shook down to disappointment after disappointment. We were always on the verge of closing in on Josefine Reiser; then something always happened and the search had to be started all over.

174

Wilhelm's letters had become more directed toward other subjects. His business interests. My work and the people I "must know." I'd become "Dearest Doris." He was signing every letter "with love," and the entire episode had grown as distasteful to me as an old, jaded relationship.

Finally, very unhappy and disillusioned, I told Wilhelm I wanted some straight answers to my questions. He suggested we go somewhere very private—like his hotel room.

I dropped my shoulder bag on the bureau in Wilhelm's sumptuous room and stayed standing. Some climax or, more likely, anticlimax was coming, and I knew I wasn't prepared to accept it.

"Well?" I finally said.

He didn't like his back to the wall. I'd seen that at dinner. He was still angry now and making little effort to conceal it. A flickering contempt crossed his face, and I didn't understand it. After all, I'd made a simple enough request. I wanted to know what the hell he was doing.

He turned to look out the window.

"It's been—how long? Nearly a year?" I persisted.

Winter to winter. A year. He remained silent, perhaps considering. Finally, he turned to look at me, expressionless, his back rigid.

"I did not know the time hung so heavy on you, Doris," he said sarcastically. "And frankly, I would have preferred not having this discussion, not wishing," he added sourly, "to see you hurt."

He stared at me then, and his voice hardened.

"Frankly," he said bitterly, "I expected more. . . ."

"More," I repeated, feeling dense. In what sense, "more"? Inputs for the search? But I had no more facts to turn over. An offer of introduction to important people Wilhelm imagined I knew? An overt sign of gratitude on my part for his efforts? A relationship between us?

175

He seemed to come to a decision. I don't know what he saw other than bewilderment on my face, but his cold eyes narrowed, and once again, as at our very first meeting, I had the sensation of being laughed at, of being made the brunt of some private joke.

"With a great deal of trouble and the efforts of many loyal workers, as well as the outlay of a substantial amount of money, I can tell you now that I have been successful."

I failed to take this in.

He made an angry gesture and cut it off short, then stuffed his hands in his pockets and rocked back a bit on his heels, head tilted.

"Successful," he repeated. "I have located Josefine Reiser."

"Josefine . . . !"

"I have, myself, been to see her. It was a terrible neighborhood," he said thoughtfully. "Terrible," watching me closely now, but I hardly noticed, my mind filled with his revelation.

"You told her about me . . . ?" My breath felt choked. I was shocked to understand he'd actually gone to Josefine, actually told her I'd asked him to make the search. I'd so doggedly impressed on him my desire *not* to have her approached by anyone but myself.

"Oh, yes," Wilhelm was smiling coolly. "I told her why I was there. She wasn't—" he searched for the appropriate word. "She wasn't overjoyed."

I was too numb with horror and rage to comment.

"No, indeed. Not overjoyed at all," he mused. "In fact, if I can recall her precise words, they went something like this: 'I won't hear anything about anybody black. If anybody black comes near me, I'll spit in her face and call the police. If you don't get out of here, I'll call the police on you!'"

176

He removed his hand from his pocket to study the nails. "Of course," he smiled, contemplating his forefinger, "I left."

I tried to pull myself together. These spiteful words didn't matter; only facts had substance. Facts could be managed. Facts were an address and a phone number.

"Her address." My throat was so dry I could barely form the words.

He lifted bright eyes to my face and shook his head slowly.

"No, my dear, I couldn't give you that information."

There was a silence so total and so drawn out that it took on weird proportions; I felt the room starting to swing around. The longer the silence lasted, the more impossible it seemed to break it. Finally, a noisy party moved up the hall from the elevators, and their laughter jarred me from my frozen staring.

"Why not?" I was pleased to hear my voice so steady, so hard and filled with ice. "The information's mine. If you'd like," I sneered furiously, "I'll pay you for it." I reached for my bag. "How much," I asked insultingly, "do you want for your services?"

For just that second his face flared with rage. Just that, then he was in perfect control of himself again.

"I will not *give*," he stressed the word, "this information to you, my dear Doris, because it is unsuitable."

I merely stared at him.

"The woman you seek out was selling her services to truck drivers on one of Munich's most notorious street corners. For five marks a throw," he added crudely. "It would seem the predilections which produced you, my dear, twenty-eight years ago, have not deserted your dear mother.

* * *

177

"Margaret?"

The phone kept slipping from my grip, and I clutched it more tightly as if that would bring her closer and push back the confusion and grief I was battling.

"I don't believe him," I said viciously, the tears dripping down my chin.

"No," she murmured calmly. "No reason at all why you should, is there?"

"Why not?" I snapped, inconsistent, and not caring.

"Why should you? Didn't I say from the start he was just a bad movie?"

"A year!" I wailed.

"So what? It was a good year, wasn't it? Busy and productive. Good career moves. And you, hoping with every letter. What's wrong with having the pleasure of anticipation?

"It wasn't a wasted year, and exactly what have you lost, anyway?"

But she answered her own question swiftly before I could drown myself in a fresh wave of dismal self-pity.

"The right answer, just in case you don't know it, is that you haven't lost anything. If this Wilhelm really did find Josefine, which, by the way, I seriously doubt, well, then, you'll just have to find her again for yourself, won't you, but at least now you know she's alive.

"And if he didn't really find her, then none of the rest's true either, so at the very worst it's a clean new start.

"Anyway," she said briskly, "you wouldn't have moved on a definite address right off, because of Louise, now would you?"

But I'd avoided that thought. Until I had some real facts, it had been easy enough to avoid future realities.

"But what do I do now?" I whispered dismally. "How can I start all over again? After all, if it *is* true, and there's no reason for Wilhelm to lie, so it must be the truth, how can I find her again to approach her again with the same result?

178

And if it isn't true, then why all the letters, the leading me on . . . ?

"He obviously wanted something back," Margaret said. "Most people do, don't they? Maybe he has some big deals cooking and when he found out you were in the media he thought you'd have some high-powered contacts that could benefit him. And maybe he expected you to offer them up on a silver platter, out of gratitude.

"Or maybe," she added flatly, "he had some different fantasies. Some nice bedroom scenes with a 'celebrity.'"

I heard her out, in silence, feeling very much alone. Oh, not physically. I *had* a roommate for company, Sharon Dorr, and friends like Toni to be with. But they couldn't help me, not *real* help, any more than Margaret could. This was just a continuation of my lifelong problem, and I had to solve it myself, or simply determine to leave it unresolved.

"If he didn't really find her, or if he found her and the rest isn't true, why would he lie to me and tell me an awful story like that? Even if it was *all* true, why did he get such mean pleasure out of dumping it on me tonight?"

"Why, to hurt you, of course." Margaret sounded surprised I'd even ask. "For disappointing him in *his* fantasy, whatever it was."

I understood about broken fantasies.

Nothing changed at WNEW. I stayed the utility player. I pushed bitter disappointment to a back shelf in my thoughts and threw myself harder than ever before into my work. Because I was a freelancer, I took on pretty much what I wanted, and for that time of my life I wanted *no* time for introspection.

But my true career goal was to anchor the news, and it became clear I wouldn't do that full-time at WNEW, no matter how much I took on or how perfectly I showed.

When I heard, in 1980, that Anna Bond was leaving

179

WABC I was hotly interested. A "right move" again, and this time I got myself a high-powered agent to handle things professionally.

Well, the timing was right again. I got the job, though not as an anchor. And before I officially started at WABC, something else momentous happened.

I met Raphael Bazin.

I'd come to New York in 1975, and I'd met a lot of men and dated without commitments on either side. By 1980, I was stuck in a slot. I was emotionally detached, and I'd almost come to believe that my career, not a husband and children, would fill my life.

I see so clearly now why I didn't trust myself to men. I couldn't bear the lost control. I valued my independence too much, because my ego wasn't safe with anybody else. I was afraid of being irrevocably hurt.

Then, too, I was terrified of really falling in love. Of *wanting* to marry and have children. I'd held firm to the decision that I *couldn't* have children without knowing my own heritage and what I might pass on.

The summer of 1980 was another transition period. I was finishing up with WNEW and looking forward to starting at WABC, where the potential seemed virtually unlimited. For the past five years, I'd been dating consistently older men, at least fifteen years my seniors. My standards were getting tougher, and I was rejecting dates from anyone failing to meet my marriage criteria: My dates had to be mature; had to be successful in their fields; had to work in jobs totally different from my own; had to be personally self-confident and secure.

Of course, I didn't seriously expect anyone to meet such criteria.

I told myself I needed someone ambitious, even driven. Someone capable of outrunning me if that's what *he* needed.

I had to know he'd never crumble, knuckling under. I had to believe I wouldn't be allowed to become a twister like my mother.

It was unfortunate that my career successes had failed to soothe my deepest personal wounds—all the emotional problems that had followed me up the road from Omaha still nipped at my ankles. I had bad dreams about my childhood—shadowy symbols I didn't understand no matter how conscientiously I tried to unravel them. Over the years of my sojourn in New York, there'd been periods of vague lurking depression. I usually attributed these to exhaustion, but I accepted exhaustion as part of my job, so I was caught in a vicious cycle of my own choosing.

I'd been doing "Black News" at WNEW. It aired Saturday nights, and we did field-shooting Wednesdays. The Wednesday that was to change my life found me at Randall's Gallery, covering an exhibit.

October 1, 1980. We were doing our feature on a Haitian artist named Luce Turnier. When the formal interview was over, Luce asked if I'd like to see more of her work back at the apartment she was sharing with a friend throughout the exhibit. I was personally interested in her style and drawn by her warmth, so we set a date for Friday, on my lunch hour.

I arrived a little early. Luce's roommate told me Luce was held up by a business appointment. I was more than normally tired, and I had to get back to work in an hour. Unreasonable annoyance pricked. I shouldn't have come at all. Sinking deeper into a black mood, I finally kicked off my shoes and dropped down on the couch and curled my legs up under myself.

That's how Luce found me. She wasn't alone. She'd brought the business appointment home.

I don't know what he saw when he came in the door. I

was sprawled and barefoot, my hair pushed haphazardly back from my face, every muscle exhausted.

What *I* saw was hardly a blow to the heart—a middle-aged man, a bit shorter than average, dressed in a blue suit and a pale silk shirt, and carrying with him a general air of superiority. He was there to pick up work he'd commissioned from Luce, but from the second he entered the apartment, he fixed me with a steady, unblinking stare.

I sat up and put on my shoes.

Luce left the room to get the paintings. The man, whose name was Raphael Bazin, stood quite still for a very long minute, then slipped his wallet from his jacket and extracted a card he presented without comment.

A business card. I stared at it, trying not to laugh at the formality of the gesture. I felt very tired. I made a great effort to come to full consciousness and behave myself.

Dr. Raphael Bazin. That's what the card said. Orthopedic Surgeon. Brooklyn, New York.

He stood silent for another moment, while I turned the card around and around in my hand. When he spoke, his voice was quiet—a nice voice; it had a comforting, self-assured sound.

"Perhaps you'll have lunch with me one day."

I stared at him. The dull weariness cleared off like a shot. Half-mocking, to cover a sudden confusion of emotion, I whipped out my own business card from WNEW.

"Maybe," I said.

He accepted the card without comment; then we proceeded to look through Luce's collection. He told me he was Haitian, that he collected Haitian art. He was pleased to find we liked many of the same pieces. For my part, I didn't understand how alert I suddenly felt. How aware of the man beside me. The longer we talked the more convinced I became that any future meetings between us would be dangerous.

182

Dr. Raphael Bazin, Orthopedic Surgeon, Brooklyn, New York, upset my equilibrium.

He wasn't at all easy to read. I sensed he wouldn't be easily dismissed either. He amused me and annoyed me for reasons I couldn't assess. I was sure he'd call me, and I knew if he did, I'd better cut him off without encouragement or else . . . ?

I told myself coldly that he wasn't at all my type. That I preferred to go on just as I was—no commitments, no recriminations. If I'd wanted to pretend to stronger feelings for any man, I'd been dating a possible candidate for months. The man I called my Black Prince was the perfect companion and undemanding friend.

But Raphael? Raphael didn't fit in my plans.

"You'd be surprised how disapproving the Haitian community would be," Raphael said over lunch the following week. "The custom in our country is to mourn for a loved one for at least a year before becoming seriously involved with anyone else."

It was an amazingly bald and sudden statement, suggesting things, as it did.

I merely raised one eyebrow and ate my chicken salad thoughtfully.

I was feeling seriously aggravated with myself for agreeing to the lunch. I certainly hadn't intended it, but when I heard his voice on the phone all previous thoughts dispersed. I was beginning to get angry, too, as Raphael proceeded to grill me mercilessly over coffee. How did I feel about children? About marriage? About careers for women? It was clear I was essentially being interviewed, but Raphael had forgotten to mention reasons.

After a while, though, his talk turned to himself. He told me about his first marriage and his wife's death, from cancer. He talked about his daughters—Manushka and Natasha. His voice changed as he related their childish escapades, and his face went dreamy, recalling shared family experiences.

And I had a news flash, sudden and searing. Raphael's voice went "buzz" and the room disintegrated.

I was going to marry Raphael Bazin in the very near future.

Absurd. Another idiotic fantasy. I didn't even *want* to, did I?

TWELVE

I STARTED MY NEW job at WABC on October 20, and the normal period of adjustment was made all the more difficult by Raphael, who'd decided to do some old-fashioned courting. Flowers started arriving not only at the apartment, but also, to my intense embarrassment, at the studio.

Too much for the new girl. I was flattered, yet put off at the same time. I wanted my transition smooth, not a flower-strewn path, and I explained this in detail while Raphael merely smiled, rethinking his campaign. Starting the next day he confined himself to doubling the arrivals at the apartment.

I gave him a hard, hard way to go. He ignored it. I half-wanted to scare him off. I had enough inner conflicts. Too many unmet personal needs to deal with a man who made me feel such new and unsettling things.

November 6 was my twenty-ninth birthday. Sharon Dorr was still my roommate. She knew about Raphael, of

185

course. She had to crawl through his floral offerings. She thought it was hilarious—easy for her to laugh. I was the one with the problem.

Two weeks before my birthday, Sharon asked me what I'd buy if I was rolling in surplus money. Well, I'd always known how I'd start spending my first million, and I fell nicely into the game, pulling out all the stops—after all, it was just a fantasy and I was good at fantasy. I put my imagination into it, all the psychic energy I hadn't dared expend on my dreams of Josefine since the episode with Wilhelm Shuster.

I didn't know that Sharon was in league with Raphael, or that she called him the next morning. Raphael didn't mention it either, when he called to tell me he'd arranged a little dinner party at the Palace Restaurant—just the two of us, Sharon, and another friend, Ellen Kaplan.

Ellen, Sharon, and I were sitting talking in the living room when Raphael arrived that evening. He was always so courteous that it shocked me considerably when he glanced at my friends, took me by the elbow, and shoved me into the bedroom.

"I know you'll excuse us," he announced, closing the door in their faces, then turning to me and groping in his jacket pocket.

"Happy birthday." He extended a tiny box that could hold only one thing.

The whole apartment was too quiet. As if Sharon and Ellen were pressed beyond the door and the rooms themselves were breathless. Winter, closed windows, no traffic sounds either, not even the heat clicking.

I stared at the diamond ring, turning it to catch the light. I knew damn well it was an engagement ring, and I felt utterly helpless. He watched me, then took the ring and reached for my left hand, and I hesitated, then thrust out my right, staring fixedly at him. For his part, he studied me in silence. Then he acquiesced and slipped the ring where I wanted it. No commitment yet.

I suppose dinner was wonderful. I have the fleeting impression the bill came to just under a thousand dollars. I don't think I can be blamed for not being sure. I didn't spend the time eating, I spent it surfacing from under the rest of Raphael's gifts.

Diamond earrings. Not the ones I'd playfully described to Sharon as part of my fantasy, but much much more elaborate. More ornate than anything I'd ever worn. They numbed me, just looking at them. And finally, a gold chain, not my dreamed-of diamonds by the yard, but a *long, long* gold chain, elaborately worked, with a separate diamond at each linking.

If it had been less, I could have dealt with it. As it was, it was so much, so very much *too* much, that I wasn't even capable of understanding the enormousness of it.

Later, understanding, I felt really helpless.

I ran the fastest race of my life for the next few weeks. Not physically. Emotionally. I fled from the solid reality of Raphael to the utter noncommitment of the man I privately called my "Black Prince." I'd dated the Black Prince fairly steadily, for longer than I'd dated anyone else. He wasn't any more interested in permanent involvements than I was, so I'd held on to this undemanding relationship.

After my Cinderella birthday dinner, I continued seeing the Black Prince. It's clear to me now that I was snatching hysterically at the status quo, terrified of taking a real, definitive forward step toward maturity.

I finally made myself look long and hard at the Black Prince, trying to tell myself I needed nothing else. He was really pretty perfect, wasn't he, all things considered? He was the right age and storybook handsome. Rich. That too. Complete with all the trimmings. If he'd given any sign, no matter how slight, over the months of our dating that he might ever grow up, might ever consider anything of more importance than himself . . .

But that was pointless, and dishonest besides. I *knew* the Black Prince, and I knew what to expect from him in a relationship, and the truth was that what he was willing to give was precisely what I'd wanted. My emotional life, since I'd met Raphael, had swerved clear off the established, comfortable, dead-end track, and Raphael's ring was still decorating the wrong hand two weeks after my birthday dinner while I tried to grow up.

One morning I woke so confused and agitated that I knew I'd run out of time for procrastinating. I considered giving back the ring and saying goodbye to Raphael and was appalled at the emptiness the thought of it gave me. Then I took the other tack and saw myself with the Black Prince, showing him the ring and telling him I was engaged, then saying goodbye to *him*. Over that, I felt nothing but a vague regret.

I had dinner with my Black Prince that night. It was one of his evenings to overwhelm, quiet and expensive. I wondered if there'd been anything in my attitude lately to make him think I needed some extra strokes.

As sometimes happens, I made an instant decision, surprising even myself.

"I'm getting married," I announced, shoving my dinner around on my plate.

"Hah," he said, cutting a chunk off his steak and chewing it thoughtfully, watching me.

"No 'hah' about it," I retorted, twisting the ring off my finger and flipping it in front of his face.

He eyed it in silence, forked up some peas, didn't comment.

I slid the ring slowly onto my left hand and studied its new position.

188

"I suppose," he waved his fork vaguely in the air, "you want some kind of commitment from me, and this is your ultimatum?"

I stared at him. "No. I don't want any commitment from you. You're not capable of commitments. You're a conceited ass, aren't you?" I asked, greatly illuminated. Then I dove into my own dinner with the first real appetite I'd felt in the past two weeks.

With that decision I stopped even pretending to understand myself. I realized—little light bulb in my head—that I'd already spent my entire life analyzing my every gesture and thought, and to little discernible purpose.

One thing *was* certain where Raphael was concerned. It made me feel terrific to know how much I was wanted. And if, at times, he was something of a male chauvinist, despite all his obvious pride in my career accomplishments, and if he did, in fact, have ready-made children who'd naturally compare me to their own mother—well, it was a challenge. I wanted to believe I didn't run from challenges.

That this one—instant motherhood—was a big one, I never doubted. I'd always given myself the excuse, over the years, that I couldn't have children of my own because I was ignorant of my own heredity. I'd liked the high tone of that—after all, what responsible adult irresponsibly endangers children? It was possible some terrible disease ran in my natural parents' families.

But now, faced with being a mother and, at the same time, deprived of excuses, I had to deal with a greater reality. I was forced to face the unflattering fact that I believed myself incapable of true motherhood.

Where would I find the instincts? I had no role model to pattern myself after. My experiences as a daughter were all either negative or confusing. I knew all the hurtful, ugly things to avoid, without knowing *how* to avoid them, and the pretty little images I labeled "mother-daughter love" were, I was sure, alien to my nature and certain to be denied to me.

Wasn't it likely I'd hear Mom's viciousness in my own voice when Raphael's girls needed discipline? That I'd hear myself say the first nasty, ugly thing that came into my head? Or, just as bad, would I take the opposite extreme and never discipline the children at all out of the fear I'd be abusive?

I'd read that. Abused children tend to become abusive parents.

Feeling desperate, battling it all out inside my own head, I assured myself that from a cold-blooded, rational viewpoint, I shouldn't be marrying Raphael. We'd certainly fight endlessly over how to raise his girls. We'd fight, for that matter, over the demands of my career, over the shortage of quality family time—he'd probably throw his first wife in my face to punish my shortcomings. . . .

But here I stopped myself, feeling ridiculous. If "cold-blooded" reasoning was my goal, it bore looking at from the other direction as well. After all, Raphael met all my marriage criteria. He was older than I was, successful, and established as an orthopedic surgeon, interested in a field totally unlike and unrelated to my own, and more: He'd shown me a romantic if dogged nature that seemed to balance and complement the emotional temerity that had marked all my earlier relationships.

I was suddenly mortally tired of myself. Some long-held rigidity fractured and let go. I'd take the big chance and try the full gamut of emotions, and if I was wrong, I'd know it soon enough.

We planned to be married early in June, and the months in between were frantic. I refused to give any thought to the speed of it all, but in the silent hours of night the doubts would creep in to taunt me. I think at some point I decided it was too damn late to turn back and escape my decision, even if I wanted to.

Raphael represented solid security to me, but he also meant responsibility. Raphael had those two little girls to call me Mommy, and that particular fear ballooned close to phobia. I knew damn well I wasn't equipped to deal with my career *plus* that reality. And yet, I was also fully aware that happiness depended to a tremendous extent on learning I was better with Raphael's girls than Louise had ever been with me.

I'd reached a fuzzy focus in my life, fixated on these thoughts of motherhood. Before, I'd viewed it only from my own side in the battles with Louise. Now, I had to turn the view around. *I'd* be "Mom." I'd do some things wrong—everybody did. And the girls would view *me* from just one side—daughters—until they, in turn, were grown up, too, and facing this same life trauma.

What did they think about? I couldn't remember my own thoughts at their ages—four and seven. Were they remembering their own mother, their "real" mother, Martine, and secretly resenting my presence? But they needed a mother now, not vague and swiftly fading memories. My God, how I could understand living on imagined love instead of having the real thing!

One day, I simply asked. It was the smart, obvious thing.

"Nuka, what do you think about my marrying your father?"

Such a grave, straight stare for a little girl. So mature. Studying me intently, then smiling a little at *my* need for reassurance.

"I think you'd be good for Daddy," she said quietly. "And we love you and we need a mommy."

We need a mommy. . . .

I think that simple statement gave me courage to be

191

straightforward, myself, for that's when I resolved to tell Raphael about Josefine and Wilhelm. I hadn't before. I'd been too filled with hot shame over the whole incident. All the while I was talking, I could hardly breathe for the tight anxiety of praying for the sort of emotional backup I needed.

"I stopped talking about Josefine after that," I admitted to Raphael. "I withdrew into myself where it was safe. What Wilhelm said was so totally in keeping with what Mom had always told me that I couldn't just dismiss it no matter how much I hated it.

"And now, if I leave it and never do another thing to try to find Josefine, this is the 'truth' I'll be left with and I'll never really be sure of anything.

"But if I do try to pursue it . . ."

"You may confirm that it's true," Raphael finished the thought for me.

I was silent.

"Would you rather know, or simply be afraid of knowing definitely?" he finally asked.

"I was never afraid, before Wilhelm, of the truth!" Easy statement, but less so when I considered it honestly. I had waited an awfully long time to initiate a half-hearted search that would still, today, enrage Louise. If Louise's feelings and mood swings were all that really counted in the past, why had I given Wilhelm the go-ahead at all? And if Louise wasn't the whole reason for my procrastination, was it possible I really didn't want to find Josefine? That I was too afraid of the truth to face it, after all?

"Have you always truly believed you'll find her?" Raphael asked.

"Yes." It was a safe answer. Truth and fantasy were too hopelessly muddled now ever to separate them out.

"And do you feel, in your heart, that she's a prostitute, as your mother and this Wilhelm said?"

"No. Of course not. At least—no. I never let myself believe that when *Louise* said it. Now . . ." I looked at him doubtfully.

"Then don't start believing it now," Raphael said simply. "Because I find that your instincts are remarkably good, and this shouldn't be an exception."

He grinned at me, and the constriction was gone from my chest. Maybe I'd fallen into the habit of taking myself too seriously. Maybe I didn't have to ask all these deep questions about my motives and thoughts. Maybe I could just live day to day, like everybody else.

"We'll find your Josefine Reiser and she'll be a middle-aged little German lady, a secretary or a teacher. Something so ordinary . . ."

And so I was back, in some measure, to the fantasy, but with the advantage of knowing Raphael would encourage me to find all the answers. I had no choice now and perhaps I never really had, for whatever it is that matures as a girl moves toward womanhood, changing her primary role from daughter to mother, whatever that facet of character involves hadn't yet developed. My daughter role was never sorted out, and that step was vital if I wasn't to shortchange Raphael's daughters. And I didn't know any way to achieve this maturity short of presenting myself back to Josefine, since I still couldn't talk to Louise about my needs and fears and self-doubts.

She wouldn't hear me. She never had.

I was learning a lot about Raphael over those weeks and months. First and foremost, that he was a mood-changer, like my mother. Not sheer nuts, like Louise, but his moods could swiftly go gold-to-black. He could be cold and unforgiving. He was totally immersed in his own career. And while it pleased him to know I was a person in my own

193

right, he also wanted a full-time wife and mother for his children.

The closer we came to our wedding day, the clearer it became that this would not be a calm union. Interesting and filled with surprises, yes. Safe? Never!

Then, two months before the wedding, which was set for June 6, I started getting phone calls. Disgusting, anonymous, the threats were directed at me, and the accusations at Raphael. I was badly shaken and totally unsuccessful in telling myself that it never paid to believe anonymous messages. I had no experience with such things; I'd certainly never received them before the announcement of our marriage. It was impossible to comprehend the sort of hatred behind them.

I didn't know that Raphael was getting similar communications in the form of anonymous letters that made all kinds of accusations against me.

On May 9, 1981, Raphael's daughter, Manushka, had her First Holy Communion. The phone calls to me, the letters to Raphael, our attempts, each of us, to pretend it didn't matter and to keep the anguish to ourselves, and finally, our understandable failure to make this work culminated that weekend.

The affair Raphael had planned for his daughter was enormous and, from my perspective, out of all normal proportion. It was very much like his overly generous birthday presents. I disapproved in silence; this was none of my business. Raphael had told me that Nuka's dead mother, Martine, had wanted a big affair, and he was merely carrying out her wishes. But I believed that part of the show was an offering to Martine—a proof that Raphael's new marriage didn't jeopardize her daughters.

Well, May 9 didn't go down in my memory or in Raphael's as the day of Manushka's Holy Communion. It

194

took its place in family history as a day of bitter battle, which was, itself, a continuation of the fight we'd been waging since Friday morning.

Raphael had finally blurted out about the letters. I was shocked, then mortally offended. Then I lost control in the face of his "Inquisitor" role and countered lamely with *my* anonymous phone calls. Between the two of us, we said a lot of ugly, hurtful things behind the locked door of his home office. Holding it in for all those weeks had given strength to the whispers.

Into this slinging of accusations trotted another grievance. Raphael had presented me, two weeks before, with a totally unexpected prenuptial agreement.

We'd been at dinner. The atmosphere between us had been strained for some time, but we'd both shuddered away from revealing our misery. It sounded so disloyal to give credence to anonymous filth by even mentioning its existence, which, of course, merely allowed the tiny seeds of doubt to grow and make us both helplessly suspicious.

"I don't believe this." I'd sat and stared at the agreement form without comprehension, my appetite gone, trying to stay cool and reasonable. Into every thought skulked the choking memory of those sneering phone calls. Taken in context, this "agreement," with all it implied, was the last straw. I couldn't bear it.

I looked at Raphael. He was picking at his food, not looking at me.

"You want me to sign a prenuptial agreement?" I asked the overly obvious. My face felt hot.

He gazed at me, vaguely, then shrugged.

"Is something wrong?" His voice was dull and remote.

"Wrong?" I tried to laugh. "What's up, Raphael? Do you think I'm marrying you for your money?"

His mouth twisted for a second, and he didn't answer; I

stared at him blankly. Then I put the paper down on the table.

"Is that what you think?" I persisted, glaring across the candles, my throat constricted.

"These things are simply the proper way of doing business," he said flatly.

"Business?" I nearly spit. *"Business?"*

For the first time in years, I'd felt that slogging in my chest. Not even the phone calls had managed that. It startled and appalled me and forced me to make a super effort to stay calm and collected. I took a breath and temporized.

"I'll consult my attorney on this." For the life of me, I couldn't put a note of lightness in my voice. We'd finished dinner, and the evening, very early.

"Was this the reason?" I asked Raphael in his house on that Communion weekend. "Were these letters and their accusations what prompted that ridiculous, degrading prenuptial agreement? Was that the full extent of your trust, that you couldn't even *talk* to me about it . . . ?"

"As *you* trust *me*?" he sneered, and with very good reason, it seemed, considering my own reticence.

Most of my clothing had already been brought to the house. That day of Manushka's Communion, I grimly sent a load of it, via a guest, back to my apartment. Then I sat and cried in the bathroom, vacillating between hysterical fury at Raphael's attitude and anguish at the loss I was already experiencing.

Finally, I closeted myself in the master bedroom and sat in the chair by the window. I stared out at the woods surrounding the house and felt cold and desolate. For no apparent reason at all, I started remembering my mother and father battling. I saw the passions of their marriage for the first time as an adult and wondered numbly if there'd been shared, private laughter, too, all of it irrevocably lost.

I knew I could follow my clothing out of Raphael's life. It

would be very easy. We weren't even started. In some ways, it would even be a genuine relief. It would resolve some of the emotional upsets I'd been facing in the dark. I could end it all now, on the basis of this weekend, putting so much of the blame on him for his failure to believe in me.

I could do that—I could run away, like my mother, from emotional commitment.

"Raphael."

He was sitting at his desk, his back to the door, his face to the wall. His shoulders were stiff, and he didn't turn his head as I came into the room and softly shut the door.

I waited in silence, not knowing how to start.

After a bit, he turned to face me. The shadows were lengthening, and maybe it was my imagination that he looked ill and desperately weary.

I found my voice.

"Do you believe it? All that . . ." I gestured toward his desk where the letters had been. They weren't there now. I had no idea what he'd done with them.

He didn't answer me, his face expressionless.

"If you do . . . Just tell me. Do you believe it?"

"You," he said harshly, "believed the phone calls."

"No," I said, sharply. "I didn't believe them. They only hurt me. And I didn't know how to tell you about them without it sounding like an accusation."

"This is not a good way to start a marriage," he said.

I laughed sharply at this absurd understatement, and he turned half away from me.

"Raphael," my voice shook. "Do you believe what's in those letters?"

"And you," he snapped, "do you believe the ridiculous lies they told *you*? No," he shook his head. "You allow

197

yourself to be *hurt!* You don't simply dismiss it all for the degenerate filth it was. . . ."

"Neither did you," I said, and my voice shook.

We stared at one another through the gloom.

"My dear . . ." he said, hands clenching.

"Raphael . . ." His face, the room, were a single gray blur. "We don't really *know* each other yet. Is it so terrible that we both let ourselves be hurt?"

"My dear," he said again, and I heard the desperate unhappiness in his voice. He was usually so self-possessed that his bitter misery now was all the more terrible. He was capable of such unbridled happiness that his pain was like the pain of a child. I couldn't bear it. I felt I'd never bear his pain lightly.

I was shivering. I didn't want to understand how much I loved him. Not now, certainly, when I might never touch him again.

But he stood abruptly and the chair whacked the wall and he came halfway around the desk, gesturing and muttering incomprehensibly in French. I put out both hands to stop him. There was one more thing I had to say.

"I can't sign the prenuptial agreement, Raphael. If it's really that important to you . . . If you can't trust that I love you . . . Please try to understand how I feel. . . ."

He took both my hands in his. "Hush," he said.

The marriage took place, as arranged. My dad and his family stayed at Raphael's house in Great Neck, and I had my secretary, Martha, reserve a hotel room for Mom and Grandma on Central Park South. To have them at the house, too, would have been the height of imbecility. All I had to remember was the night of my graduation, and the way Mom had reacted to Lena's presence.

I hadn't expected Mom to be pleased, but that didn't stop her phone call from upsetting me.

198

"I don't want to stay here," she said flatly. They must have just arrived. Walked in, tipped the bellman. Made right for the phone. They certainly hadn't had time to unpack.

"You don't put family in hotel rooms," Mom added coldly. "You put family in your home."

"I have a roommate. You know that. The apartment's not big enough for anyone to stay over. I told you." I was gripping the phone too tight.

"There's always room," she pronounced grimly; I could picture her sitting stiff on the edge of a chair. "If you really want somebody."

I knew that from her point of view this was true. Hell, look at the herd of people always in and out of Grandma's and Aunt Ruth's.

"The apartment's too small for company," I said, putting cool reason into my tone.

Error.

"Company? *Company?*"

I sighed, but every muscle was tightening up. The air I tried to suck in should have given me balance, but I couldn't seem to get enough to make a difference.

"You know perfectly well what I mean," I said.

"Of course I know perfectly well what you mean," she snapped. "You see us as company, here for *your* pleasure. It doesn't matter to you how far we had to come for the 'privilege' of seeing you marry a man old enough to be your own father."

"Mom, please . . ."

Her breath was coming heavy over the wire. Her voice had gone flat and monotonous. A drone, barrier against understanding.

I could see disaster looming, with the victim, predictably, me.

"I won't let you do this to me," I stated flatly, my heart

slogging into my throat and back down. "This is my *wedding* we're talking about, Mom, not some little party we can have again some time. Can't you try to just be happy for me and not make things harder. . . ."

"Harder?" she mocked. "Harder? You finding marrying this old man a hard thing to do, Doris? Well, you surprise me. I didn't think you'd ever do anything that wasn't your pleasure of the moment."

I sucked air again and tried to count to ten and couldn't remember how. Literally, couldn't remember how to count to ten, my mind an ugly blank, my own anger rising.

"Can't you be happy for me?" I repeated, my throat tight.

Silence. Long, total, and deadly.

"Mom . . . ?"

Nothing.

Finally, I hung up the receiver.

Friday evening was the dress rehearsal. It was also the first contact between Mom and Dad and Lena. Mom was surprisingly haughty, keeping her thoughts to herself, disconcertingly watching every step I took. Her attitude toward Raphael was one of intense dislike. This was sudden. When she'd learned of our engagement, she'd been pleased and encouraging. Reality seemed to have strung her up tight.

Raphael was surprised and a little hurt, then advised me to let it go. He'd grown quite introspective, and I realized with some shock that night of the dress rehearsal that he was as frightened of the marriage as I was myself. Guilt, perhaps, over not waiting a full year after Martine's death? Lingering doubts about the anonymous notes?

Saturday morning was our wedding day—a full day of ceremony. I put on a white suit. Pulled back my hair. Put on a minimum of make-up. Hopped into a limousine with

200

four friends—Toni Jones, my maid of honor; Charlotte Scott Bell, my matron of honor; my roommate, Sharon; and my secretary, Martha. It was a nagging sadness at the back of my thoughts that Margaret, of all people, had ended up not making it. She'd had an operation and could barely walk.

Raphael was Catholic, and despite Mom's efforts throughout my childhood, I'd decided I wasn't. I was a Baptist like my Dad, and I'd found an inner core of strength in my faith. We'd therefore agreed to two ceremonies, the first at Saint Aloysius Church, in Great Neck, the second at Tavern on the Green. Dad and his family came to the Catholic ceremony, but I didn't invite Grandma or Louise Evelyn. I was afraid Mom would make a scene.

I was certain she'd mortally embarrass me as she had at my college graduation. I wanted only to put things off as long as I could, a coward's act that made little sense since the larger ceremony at Tavern on the Green was better for a display of histrionics—it was so much more public, the audience so much bigger.

Mom showed up at my apartment building later, after the church ceremony. John Prapolenis was finishing my hair. The Channel 7 make-up artist, Marilyn Peoples, was ready to leave. I wanted everything absolutely perfect for this ceremony. I wanted nothing but good omens for Raphael's and my future together.

I didn't even know when Mom arrived. She chose to stay downstairs, outside the lobby. She was in her element there, entertaining my waiting friends. Raving and ranting about how she'd been mistreated and how she wasn't even sure she was going to the ceremony.

That's where I found her when I was ready to leave. I was beautifully dressed, made up, and coiffed, and wondering if she was about to jump in my face.

201

"I'm going home," she said, not looking at me. "Won't matter to you, you've got everybody in the world here anyway, I'm just extra. . . ."

I felt so tired. There'd been so much pain. Even my fantasy had turned to pain, though I kept trying for fresh optimism because I felt it was necessary.

"You'll have to do what you want. Go or stay. You will anyway, no matter what I say. I won't beg you," I told her wearily, aware she wanted just that. It might have been revealing if I'd cared to take the time to work it out. Mom, wanting assurance of *my* love.

She turned to stare at me. I couldn't see her expression. She was wearing huge sunglasses, ugly as sin, that masked her whole upper face.

"It would have been nice," she said with stiff dignity, "if I could have thought I was special to you, if your inviting me was special, not just a group invitation."

It wasn't like her. Her voice was trembling. I tried to bring her into full focus, push myself out, and found it was impossible. This was *my* day. Mine and Raphael's.

I felt tight all over, pain starting in my head. I knew from experience there was no way this conversation could possibly go but to the devil.

"I won't argue this with you," I said flatly. "I can't do that to myself or to Raphael. I can't let you ruin this for me the way you ruined my graduation and so much else."

Her hand came up in protest, then fell, and she turned away. I took a step toward her, then made myself stop, my throat tight, my face hot, tears threatening. Something seemed to break in my chest.

"Can't you just once feel joy for me?" I wailed. "Just once think of me first, and wish me happiness?"

There was a long silence. When she turned toward me, I was shocked by the trembling of her hands as she pushed at the sunglasses. She moved past me then, careful not to touch, and took herself away off down the street. And until I reached Tavern on the Green and saw her sitting silent and alone, I didn't even know if she'd be at my wedding.

I remember the pictures. They were a terrible ordeal. The same poses being created and recreated ad nauseam and Raphael telling me it would be over soon and that someday I'd thank him for making me take the trouble.

Mom and Lena in the same photo with me. Standing shoulder to shoulder behind me where I sat, not looking at one another or speaking. Mom, refusing to remove those atrocious sunglasses, murmuring, almost inaudibly, that she had an eye infection. Mom, in my wedding pictures, caught there forever, with those sunglasses hiding eyes I saw un-shielded only once, later. Red eyes that had cried great tears whose cause wasn't confided in me.

She came to me, back at the house, later that afternoon. She touched my arm, in a crowd, and when I turned I saw she'd finally removed the sunglasses.

There was no anger or resentment, just resignation in her tone. It made her words nonsensical.

"I'll never step foot in this house again."

I was tired and about finished, and my vague thought was that she wanted attention. I was silent, finding nothing kind to say, and finally she put the sunglasses back on and I didn't see her again that day.

Raphael and I left for a two-week honeymoon in Tahiti. Summer passed. I didn't hear from Mom and didn't initiate a conversation.

In August, she called.

"I thought I should tell you," she said unemotionally. "I'm going into the hospital next week. I have a lump in my breast."

203

THIRTEEN

THE ROOM WAS VERY quiet. All the chairs were full. Mr. Murphy stood by the window, though he'd been sitting in a borrowed white folding chair before. He hadn't spoken a word in all the hours I'd been there.

Grandma slumped in the green padded chair that belonged to the room. Aunt Ruth had planted herself in its twin, which belonged, technically, to Mom's roommate, who was heavily sedated and without visitors.

I hovered at the bedside, wandered out in the hall, roamed up and down, and felt helpless and scared.

Mom lay in the bed looking desperately ill. Tubes from her arm, a drainage bag from her chest—she'd vomited twice, not really awake yet.

"Louise."

Aunt Ruth tried it periodically, without success.

"Wake up, darlin', it's over, everything's fine now, wake up, Louise."

Fine! A mastectomy.

There was a virulent hiss from the bed. Mom opened both eyes and stared unseeing at the ceiling. "Be still, Ruth," she mouthed. "You'll wake up Mrs. Smith."

We all gaped at her, then at her roommate, then back at Mom, but she sighed heavily, fingers plucking at the sheet covering her, and slept.

"Will you help me, Doris?"

I'd been waiting to help her, to feel like her true daughter, all my life. Her voice was disembodied, coming as it did from the tiny bathroom where she'd gone, minutes before, to try to urinate. It was the day after the surgery; she'd insisted on getting up at noon and walking up and down in the hallway. She'd been to the bathroom several times, but the smallness of the cubicle made her dizzy and nauseated.

The toilet seat, she said, murmuring so as not to bother her roommate, was frigid.

I went to the doorway of the bathroom, hesitant and surprised. No one else had come yet. Visiting hours weren't officially started.

Mom stood in the bathroom, in front of the sink. There was the tiniest imaginable mirror in there, and she was trying to step back far enough to see her upper self in it.

"Help me with this gown, Doris," she said quietly.

"Mom . . ."

She turned, painfully, to study my strained face. There was a long silence between us; then she shook her head.

"I'm prepared. I prepared myself. I imagined it the worst it could possibly be, before it ever happened, and now I just need to see. Help me." The command in her voice was borderline vintage Louise.

I felt my mouth twist in protest, but it was protest for myself. *I* was afraid to see. I helped her open the gown to the sides and we both stared then, in the inadequate mirror, at the butchery.

205

After a bit, she wet her lips and fumbled to close the gown. I helped her tie it.

"That gown you brought me was lovely, Doris," she murmured, pressing her hands to her sides for a minute.

I felt flushed with holding back tears. Neat incisions, neat stitching, drainage tube, just the small matter of a breast missing . . . What had she said? Gifts . . . ?

"It was a stupid gift," I said, struggling to get the words out past the aching anguish in my throat and chest. "I should have realized you couldn't put up your arms to get it over your head. I just wanted you to have something pretty. . . ." I stumbled to a dead stop, recalling the last-minute trip to Saks Fifth Avenue, the sumptuous silk Christian Dior folds I would have adored having myself.

Bribes to beg love. Sops to endless guilt.

There, in the little bathroom, it didn't even make sense. The woman I'd bought the gown for was a total stranger, someone I'd struggled without success to know for years. The woman before me was tired and shaky on her feet, in pain, vulnerable, and somehow, mysteriously, my mother. Not that stranger, Louise.

"Let me get you a better gift," I blurted, suddenly inspired. "Will you be wanting a prosthesis; did they talk to you about it . . . ?"

"Oh, I don't know about that," she followed me from the bathroom, then sat in the padded chair, with me perching on the bedside. "Somehow . . ." She gazed at me blankly. "Thank you for the offer," she said stiffly.

"Mom," I put both my hands out impulsively toward her and she hesitated, then closed them in her broader, warmer ones. For those seconds of calm silence, we were close.

She pulled herself together.

"Now, Doris," she said, a bit sharply, "don't be a silly baby, you heard what the doctor said. Good clean cut, good clean surgery . . ." Her voice faded out for a second, then came back smooth. "He thinks he's got it all, all the cancer,

206

and I'll start the chemotherapy, and you see, Doris, I've been waiting for something truly terrible, I never knew what, but something horrible I'd have to face, and I've watched for it for so long, wondering. . . ." She choked to an abrupt stop, looking as if she feared she'd revealed too much, staring at me hard to see my reaction. Whatever she saw, her face relaxed in a small smile. So rare, to have her smile.

"Well, the shoe finally dropped. I can stop being afraid."

I couldn't find anything to say. I'd never known she could *be* afraid, no matter what Dad's own interpretation of her behavior. For myself, I'd viewed her moods always from the level of a child. Even when I was older, my entire frame of reference remained just what it originally was. Mom was sometimes furious and hot, sometimes depressed and cold. What she'd never seemed to be was personally afraid of anything or anyone.

"You can go home to your family now," she added. "There's plenty of people around to keep an eye on me and the worst's over."

It was the end of the week, and next day I was going home. I came early to the hospital as I had each morning. No one had tried to stop me or confine my visits to the proper hours. These were the longest times I'd ever had alone with my mother.

She was sitting in the padded chair when I got there that morning. Her head was bent and her hands were clenched tight in her lap.

I stopped dead in the doorway. "What's wrong?" My voice was too loud in the silence.

One second she was hunched in the chair, all the brave confidence gone, then she saw me and straightened and brushed angrily at her face and abruptly stood.

The room was full of flowers and cards, and the phone

never stopped ringing. I hadn't known the extent of the friendships she'd formed. How could I?

"What's wrong?" I repeated.

"I go home tomorrow."

I didn't understand. She'd been looking forward to leaving the hospital. Everyone wants to leave hospitals.

"Don't you feel up to it?"

She turned half away.

"Would you like me to stay over a little longer, until you get settled at the house?"

And suddenly I knew what I should have known before. At home she'd be alone with her mutilated self. No hospital corridors to walk, no other patients to visit and console. Just herself and her husband, whose character and needs and emotions were a mystery to me and probably of little comfort, just then, to her. She *must* see herself altered. Less? Frightened all over again of losing things, as Dad knew long ago?

"Stay here another day," I said flatly. "Tell them you're just not ready to go. They're not bothered for space, they can easily keep you for another day or two, just tell them you don't feel ready to be on your own. They must understand the tremendous trauma you've been through, and besides"—I tried to smile—"you're their very best candy striper. None of the patients on the floor would be coming along half as well without you to cheer them up."

To my surprise, she took my advice, and stayed one more day. And I went home to Great Neck because that's what she said she wanted. She phoned me the following evening to say she'd realized her own cowardice and had gone home to face it.

Monday morning, early, became my time to call, every single Monday before her chemotherapy. The tenuous closeness that had started in the hospital miraculously continued. No more judgments from Mom—I felt I'd finally stopped performing. No more silent, hurtful expectations from me—it was past time to put away the lost needs of childhood and revel in the knowledge that we seemed capable of simple friendship.

One morning she told me, as we prepared to ring off, about her cards and well-wishers—scores of them.

"I have all my lovely cards. I put them all up on the wall. One *whole* wall of my bedroom papered with them. You wouldn't believe how beautiful they are. . . ." Her voice shook. "You wouldn't believe the love I can feel, pouring from them, out over me like a shield.

"They'll stay here," she said flatly. "They'll stay here 'til I die."

Summer pulled to autumn's brief glory; then even autumn died. I was working crazy hours at WABC and trying to domesticate myself. I couldn't have asked for a better environment to learn in, slowly and without pressure. Raphael had a cousin who looked after the children. There was a housekeeper to clean the house. My chores as wife and mother were only what I could manage.

But I'd held on to my apartment. After all, it was silly to give it up, it was so perfectly located for my work, wasn't it . . . ?

I worked the early morning shift, doing the local newsbreaks for "Good Morning America," and every Monday morning I'd call Mom between seven and seven-thirty. She appeared to be coming along okay except for the sickness she'd feel after chemotherapy.

Monday, October 5. I never did get my call through. I'd been diddling around talking to people. Then I got off the air at seven-thirty to find Raphael on the line.

"I didn't call Mom yet. I can just catch her. Let me get back to you."

I thought he was incredibly obtuse, for he stuck tight to the phone, asking the most inane questions about every-

209

thing under the sun. His sudden need for conversation made me miss my call to Mom.

My air shift ended at eight-thirty that morning. I'd been feeling exhausted and nervous, jumping at every sound.

"Doris."

I turned, startled. Raphael stood behind me. His overcoat was open; his eyes were distressed. He took me into my managing editor's office, his arm around my shoulders.

That's when I fully understood what my mother had meant about waiting for the shoe to drop. I felt the blank terror of *knowing*. Not a certainty, but worse, a coming obscenity. I had nothing to brace me but Raphael's closeness.

"I love you, Doris," he said softly. "You know that, don't you? That I'll always be here for you?"

I stared at him, frightened to utter silence.

"Your mother's taken a turn for the worse."

"What do you mean?" It was incomprehensible. She was doing just fine. The worst was over.

"There was a problem, they called. . . ."

"Who called?" I heard my voice rising. "When? Why didn't you tell me right away? My God, I didn't get to talk to her this morning. . . . Was that why you called at seven-thirty? So I'd finish up here before I heard this? You thought I couldn't handle it? Why would you think I couldn't handle it?"

"Sweetheart . . ."

"I have to call now. Where is she? At home . . . ?" I turned, fumbling, for the telephone.

He took me by the shoulders and made me look into his eyes.

"Doris. Listen to me. Your mother's dead."

FOURTEEN

I FLEW OUT TO Detroit to make the funeral arrangements. Mom had always said that she wanted to be cremated. I didn't know if she was serious, but that's what I had done anyway. Grandma and Aunt Ruth weren't thrilled about it. Grandma kept crying and asking how I could burn up her child. I felt so strange, in pain and determined, too, and I stuck to my guns. It was impossible to pretend I knew what my mother would have wanted.

The whole family was there, including cousins I'd never seen before or only rarely met. Like the distant cousin who'd taken Mom's natural daughter, Caroline, to raise, along with Caroline, herself, in the flesh.

Louise's daughter stared at me over her mother's coffin. Being given away had done nothing to mask the bloodline. There she stood, spitting image of Louise, even sounding like her. That's what pervaded every later thought—Caroline's face/Louise's face, everywhere.

Caroline stood crying and wailing, twisting her hands, acting the role of the rightful daughter of the house, if such things can be judged by measures of overt distress, while I stood frozen, all locked up inside. I hadn't yet been able to cry. I watched Caroline's histrionics over a woman she hadn't really even known and wondered if my tears would come easier if this was Josefine's funeral.

They'd dressed Mom in the pink eyelet dress she'd worn to my wedding. Somehow that parallel ripped away any hope of believing this was happening. I could not make myself understand that my mother was dead. I'd never *known* her as my mother, but friendship *had* been starting, and we'd had so much still to work out, yet she'd left me alone again, this time irrevocably.

The wake was held at the funeral home, with the funeral scheduled for the following Saturday. Dexter Avenue Baptist Church was packed. Mom had spent a lot of time and energy organizing affairs and raising money for the church. The line past the casket went on for some time. Scores of people, red-eyed and crying. I was hot and numb and couldn't shed a drop. My only thought, when I finally paused at the casket, was that it was time she got herself up. She had no business dying. There were too many things left to explain and set right. She had no business leaving me— the final rejection of my life.

After the funeral, I went back to the house with Mr. Murphy. We were alone there for a few minutes before friends and family started to arrive. I'd made up my mind to ask for any papers Mom had kept about my adoption. I felt angry. So terribly, helplessly angry.

"Mom had some things that are mine now."

Mr. Murphy looked at me blankly. It felt miserably empty at the house. Then his face cleared, and he led me past the bedroom where the wall was still papered with her treasured get-well cards. I leaned against the doorframe and closed my eyes.

He disappeared into the den, then returned with a black attaché case. He didn't bother to check the contents.

"I think this is what you're wanting, Doris." He looked at me, then handed it over, silent.

I went home with my paper fantasy to Great Neck.

BIRTH CERTIFICATE

Registrar's Office Munich-Pasing No. 526/51

Doris Elisabeth Reiser
was born on November 6, 1951 in Munich-Pasing,
Engelbertstrasse 16
Mother: Josefine Regina Reiser, clerk, Catholic
residing in Munich-Pasing, Landsbergerstrasse 382

CERTIFICATE OF BAPTISM

In the year one thousand nine hundred and fifty-one
(1951) on the 6th day of November was born in
Munich-Pasing and on the 8th day of November
1951 christened in the parish "Maria Schutz" to
Roman-Catholic Rite

Doris Elisabeth Reiser

Parents' name: Reiser   Josefine
Profession: Clerk   Residence: Munich
Religion: Catholic

DEED OF CONSENT

This day, the twenty-third of December in the year
one thousand nine hundred and fifty-two
December 23, 1952

before me, Hans Hieber, Notary Public in Munich,
appeared:
Miss Josefine Reiser, typist in Munich 42,
Landsbergerstrasse 382/o,
born on March 6, 1928 in Munich,
who proved her identity by producing her Deutsche
Kennkarte.
She requested me to draw up the following consent:

I herewith expressly and irrevocably consent that
my child

Doris Elisabeth Reiser,

born on November 6, 1951 in Munich-Pasing,
be adopted and granted the position of a legal child
by the American spouses who have already taken
care of her since December 17, 1952 and who are
listed in the records of Stadtjugendamt Munich
under No. 674/52.

I further accept that the child will solely bear the
family name of the adoptive parents and emigrate
with them.

ADOPTION CONTRACT

This day, the eleventh of March in the year
one thousand nine hundred and fifty-three,
March 11, 1953
before me, Hans Hieber, Notary Public in Munich,
Thiereckstrasse 2/I (Munich Notaries' Office No. XII)
appeared:

1.) Mr. Horace G. McMillon, Staff-Sergeant of the
State of Florida/USA

214

and his lawful wife Mrs. Louise E. McMillon, nee
Baker,

both at present in Moosburg, Stotzenbachstrasse 1,

2.) Miss Josefine Reiser, housewife in Munich,
Landsbergerstrasse 382/o
acting as guardian of the child Doris Elisabeth
Reiser, born on November 6, 1951 in Munich-
Pasing according to the certificate of
Amtsgericht–Vormundschaftsgericht–Munich Reg.
No. VII 5189/51.

Mr. and Mrs. McMillon proved their identity by
producing their Identification Cards, Miss Reiser
by producing her Deutsche Kennkarte.

At the request of these persons, simultaneously
present
I draw up the following

Contract of Adoption

THE UNITED STATES OF AMERICA
CERTIFICATE OF NATURALIZATION
Petition No. 260565

Personal Description of Holder as of Date of
Naturalization:

Date of Birth: Nov. 6, 1951   Sex: female
Complexion: dark   Color of Eyes: brown
Color of Hair: black   Height: 3 feet 0 inches
Weight: 42 pounds
Visible Distinctive Marks: none
Marital Status: single
Former Nationality: German

I certify that the description given above is true and that the photograph affixed hereto is a likeness of me.

Louise Evelyn McMillon, on behalf of Doris Elizabeth McMillon

In testimony whereof the seal of the court is hereunto affixed this 9th day of July in the year of our Lord nineteen hundred and fifty-seven and of our Independence the one hundred and eighty-second.

Detroit, Michigan, July 9, 1957

Name changed by Decree of Court from Doris Elisabeth McMillon to Doris Elizabeth McMillon as part of the Naturalization.

I studied the papers on the plane going home, and when I got there, I locked myself in my office and studied them some more. Cold facts—no fantasy surfacing here. An oddly unreal set of facts with the starring role given to me. I went over and over the papers, but more particularly the pictures in the folder, one of them that picture Dad had shown me of the headless woman—Josefine.

Not one of the pictures showed Josefine's features, but the man who appeared in several of the photos—a man in uniform I believed was my biological father—was shown full-face, smiling and whole. I realized he'd never posed any more threat to Louise than he'd seemed to hold promise for myself.

He was young and handsome and full of himself. I tried to imagine their meeting, Josefine and he, a white German woman and a black American soldier in post-Hitler Germany. They must have been ostracized for their relationship. That was the most likely reason for my adoption, of course, but I'd always managed to ignore it in my dreams.

There was no more time for romantic fantasy.

I wrote a letter to the United States Consulate in Munich on October 22, 1981. I'd lost all inclination toward procrastination. It was almost as if Mom's death had forced me to face all my responsibilities immediately. I'd gotten through the misery of arranging for the funeral, and now I had to get through this.

I explained my situation and asked for any help the consulate could give me. Then I called our ABC correspondent in Bonn, Hal Walker. He took down the facts I'd gleaned from my adoption papers.

"I see from this stuff you have a birthday coming up."

I was puzzled. "November sixth. Why?"

"I'll try to have a birthday present for you."

It was late. Dark. The bed was warm, and security was mine. If I had the courage to let it happen for me. The will to let go of some measure of absolute independence. If I could learn how to share, fully, in my marriage, without feeling that sharing meant losing a vital part of myself forever.

"What if Mom was right?"

Raphael took a long moment to answer.

"I've told you, it's absurd to let yourself believe such garbage!"

"And Wilhelm . . ."

Raphael made a small snorting sound that totally dismissed Wilhelm from consideration.

"Your friend in Munich, this Hal. You believe he'll find her for you?"

"Yes. I don't know why. I believe it."

"Then also believe that she won't be a disappointment to you. Oh," he shifted onto his elbow, "I'm not saying she'll be the fantasy lady you've imagined all your life. But not the devil of your mother's nightmares either. As I said before, something nice and ordinary, in between." He laughed. "Probably a disappointment, but not in terrible terms, only in terms of normality."

I wanted very much to believe this.

Hal didn't make it for my birthday; he was three days late.

"You're not going to believe this. She's listed right in the Munich telephone directory. It was too damn easy; if I'd thought to check there first thing, you would have had your birthday present. . . . I can give you the address and telephone number in Munich; I have it right here. . . . What? No, I'm telling you. It's absurd how easy it was. You could have found her yourself any time at all just by calling Munich information."

Then what *had* Wilhelm been up to with his "long hard search," his army of workers, his outlay of funds for information? His phone calls? His letters, leading me on and on . . .

Would I ever learn the answer? Or was it wiser just to trust Margaret's interpretation and let the memory of Wilhelm go?

I asked an acquaintance who spoke fluent German to call the number Hal gave me. To talk to Josefine Reiser, explain why she was calling, and thereby test the waters for me.

She called back that evening.

"Doris? You didn't have to worry. She speaks good English. I guess that makes sense, doesn't it? You said you think your father was an American GI. . . .

"She said she wants to see you. She said, 'Finally . . .'"

218

FIFTEEN

WABC DECIDED TO LEAD off the new five o'clock show with the story of my search, my find, my trip. . . .

"This is Julie Eckhart for Doris McMillon. As you know, she's going to Germany to meet her Mom—it's the story of a real miracle. We'll be bringing you all the details. . . ."

There was to be a film crew at the airport to see me off. There was to be a German crew waiting in Munich at the airport. It couldn't be helped—it was the nature of my job—yet I felt the wrongness of it deeply. Not so much for myself—I liked the idea of having the reunion on film to replay over and over—but for Josefine.

All those strangers would obscure our initial reactions. It was a buffer, in that sense, noise and action to fill the first empty moment when I'd look at my natural mother and she at me. It would keep things impersonal for a little while, yet I knew, in the end, that procrastination wouldn't help, but

219

only make it harder. And the moment of aloneness that had to come would be postponed, but not made easier.

Eleventh hour for me? Whatever remained of my lifelong fantasy was disintegrating rapidly. Truth was too close; I'd know it all soon. The thought was devastating.

Why *hadn't* she wanted me? Really! Why *had* she given me up? It was the end of dreaming.

III

ACORNS

SIXTEEN

My BAGS WERE FINALLY packed and it was time to go, but I still sat at my desk with the papers and pictures and more. Much, much more. James Murphy had sent me a package that arrived an hour before. I wouldn't have believed his timing could be so cruel. If he'd wanted to hurt me, he couldn't have planned it more perfectly.

Thick, heavy albums filled the mailing box. The albums were cover to cover with all the pictures and moments of my life. Not only yearbook snapshots, but notes from school, awards both big and small—every single thing ever recorded from my earliest months. Newborn photos Mom must have gotten at the time of my adoption. Even a picture of the rear end of my first car, showing its license plate number.

I'd hungered throughout life for some sign that she'd loved me and wanted me and been glad I was her child. The silent message in those albums came too late and was disastrous. The albums screamed that she'd cared beyond reason. It made the trauma of my childhood unbearable.

This was solid proof that she'd really been ill. *I* felt ill. I couldn't fully grasp the extent of emotional damage she'd suffered solely through her inability to show love and, thereby, leave herself vulnerable. I saw a mirror-image of myself in this, in the need to self-protect, and it terrified me.

I could suddenly imagine her talking to her friends. Telling them my childhood exploits, as all parents do, but always in this way—kept a careful secret from the one person who would have loved to hear the pride and exaggeration. Myself.

I could imagine she'd really loved me. . . . Imagine it? It was the one thing I'd never been able to feel. The albums, their contents, were like another, more bizarre fantasy.

And why hadn't she ever shown me the albums? Why hadn't she shown me her love? Was I to believe she simply hadn't known how, or wasn't it more likely there were deeper, more devastating explanations for how frozen up she'd been inside herself?

Sitting there, ready to start a new adventure I'd dreamed of most of my life, what I felt was the futility of everything. I felt demolished.

She'd withheld love and warmth and all the things I'd needed and desired just to protect herself because she was afraid of a ghost—Josefine Reiser. I realized the extent of her fear for the very first time. She felt that Josefine had a bond with me that she could never have because she didn't carry me. She thought that meant I wouldn't love her enough, or ever feel she was my real mother. So she threw Josefine in my face before I could even begin to imagine my own interest in my natural parents. As if being the one to instigate it would make it hurt her less.

I tried to understand this, emotionally, beyond the intel-

224

lectual. It was mind-boggling. It was sick and self-destructive. It was wrong, to put it at its most blunt and basic. It was worse to have loved and kept it a secret than not to have loved at all.

And I hadn't even needed the evidence of the albums, the glimpse of Louise's terrible caring. I hadn't needed it now, at this point in my life, for I'd already begun reordering my memories and expectations. I'd been viewing with utter lack of emotion my coming meeting in Munich with Josefine.

I'd done bitter battle in my mind about what was worth remembering and what was only selective imaginings. The change in my relationship with Mom after her surgery, the tentative start of communication between us, of a more relaxed easiness, the sharp anguish I'd felt and still felt at her death, the rage, too, most especially that, the feeling I'd been cheated—all this told me what I'd long suspected and feared.

Louise was the vital factor through my life, even if I hadn't yet defined what she'd been to me. I'd driven myself hard for her love and approval, and everything else was just dreams.

Josefine? Josefine was a total stranger, conjured up for comfort like an imaginary playmate, and I felt fear and anticipation at the meeting in Germany, but no sense of homecoming, of family. Only the knowledge of finally finishing old business.

I sat staring at the phone until it was time to go. It was too late to be sorry for starting the whole business. I had to have my answers, and Louise couldn't give them to me.

There was too much time on my flight for reevaluations. My fantasy image of Josefine did a total reversal. I saw her suddenly as no longer young and vital, certainly not the stuff of heroines and heartbreakers, but as just an aging, tired woman, still unmarried and waiting alone in a large

225

airport for a glimpse of her lost daughter. As frightened as I was. As alone with her memories and guilts. We wouldn't even know each other. How could we? I'd never seen a photograph of her face.

It was foolish to imagine there'd be natural ties. Some physical resemblance, like that shared by Louise and Caroline. Shared thoughts or likes or dislikes. How could there be? We were two total strangers, thrust together not out of love or luck but through my own pigheaded determination to prove Louise's death wasn't the end of my hope for a better image of myself.

It would be terrible. As the plane circled to land, I was sure it would be the most terrible experience of my life.

The terminal was jammed. Reporters from the German press were everywhere. The station had hired a film crew to be present at the meeting. Was Josefine even here?

But the film crew assured me she was waiting outside customs. That she'd been waiting for some time. That she wasn't alone, she was with other members of the family.

The Reiser family. My family.

Waves of heat and cold kept chasing each other from head to toe. One of the cameramen was saying something, but I couldn't understand; I'd shut down. My suitcases finally appeared, but customs took forever, and that was salvation. I didn't *want* to get through customs; I didn't want to face the woman waiting somewhere in the crowded terminal.

I wished I'd never started this. I wanted desperately to be back home.

One of the reporters kept gesturing toward the glass doors where people were waiting for arriving passengers. She kept saying something I couldn't quite catch, but it didn't matter; one of the distant women was waving at someone. I couldn't see her face—there was too much distance and distortion through the glass—but I knew it was Josefine. . . .

226

Then, finally, I was cleared. I had my luggage. I was walking toward the doors, my steps dragging, numb with fear. Then the doors wheezed open, and I was through, into much colder air and waiting crowds and her.

My mother?

She put a hand out toward my face, then drew it back. She stood and looked at me, long and hard, and touched her own cheek. This time when she reached, I stepped closer, and her arms went around me, tentative and frightened, and I felt her shivering.

"Oh God. Doris . . ."

She wasn't blond and beautiful. She certainly wasn't young. She wasn't statuesque and self-contained, or even particularly stereotypically "German."

She was about my height. She wore glasses, but she kept taking them off to rub her eyes, then jamming them back on. Her hair was short and curled and dark. There was an expression of extreme bewilderment and pain on her face.

She wore large earrings, just the kind I liked, and I imagined I saw her eyeing my own earrings, comparing them, as we walked.

Little bits of nonsense to cover up embarrassment.

Nothing important penetrated the haze. I had a growing tendency to start laughing hysterically. The reporters who'd come to cover the story were everywhere. Josefine's head bowed under their onslaught. Our story, it seemed, was to be big news in Germany.

Finally, very late, it occurred to me how drastically Josefine's life might be affected by this baring of her long-hidden indiscretion.

But she'd said, "Come." She'd wanted me. And for the moment, at least, nothing else could be permitted to matter.

"It's strange, you know? I was thinking of you, so sad, it was your birthday. Every year, but especially this year, you can ask your Tante Susie. How you were, what you looked like, grown up, and how your life turned out.

"I know you want to ask why I gave you up. No. I don't want you to say anything, Doris. Just let me talk, first. You have to understand what Germany was like. What the life was like then, after the war, when there wasn't enough of anything at all, and we grasped at the smallest hope.

"It was strange that we should have looked to the nice American soldiers for relief from such poverty.

"That's how I met your father. Ernie-boy. That's what I called him. Ernest Barnett. He was a soldier and I met him and we went out together. I suppose you'll find that hard to understand, too, considering what you must think of the social situation in Germany.

"It was not something that was approved, you understand. It was just that he was kind and generous and so my family ate well for a while and that made all the difference. And I think I even believed myself in love. I was very young then. Very innocent. Don't laugh, it's true, even though I already had a child—your half-sister, Brigitte.

"But you don't know about Brigitte yet. That's another story.

"I was very innocent still. I believed Ernest would take precautions against a child. I told him this was necessary; I couldn't even manage to support myself and Brigitte and my mother, as it was. I became very dependent on Ernest to help me, and he promised so nicely, and he bought me such beautiful things.

"A lovely dress and he took me out. Shoes to match. You can't imagine what it was like, having something I felt pretty in after all those years.

"He was a nice, gentle man, but he was a ladies' man, too, and I was too innocent and blind to understand this. I only learned how little I could really depend on him when I found I was pregnant with you.

228

"But this isn't what you wanted to hear, is it, Doris? You wanted to hear some beautiful love story. Some romantic, tragic story to explain your adoption. I thought about making something pretty up for you. But I can't, you know? You're my daughter. I think it had better be just the truth."

The reporters had finally been banished by the closing of her door. That left us alone, and she told me these things that I'd waited so long to hear. We sat facing each other in stiff, unnatural poses. The rest of the family, the Reiser family, had been introduced, but I remembered none of their names or relationships or faces.

Just Josefine. My mother.

I told her I'd fantasized her all my life. She looked surprised, then as I talked about Louise, horrified. Finally given this release, I talked and talked and couldn't stop, spitting out anguish from so deep down that it was a cramp, up my back, all through my stomach, twitching around my mouth. And after, slumped exhausted, I watched her face as *she* talked. I thought she looked familiar, then knew, tingling hot, that it was *her* features I saw when I examined myself in my mirror.

Something to do with the shape of her head. Her chin and jaw. Definitely the odd creases in the skin of my neck. I had the notion I'd inherited the shape of her legs as well, but I couldn't very well ask her to stand up and let me have a look.

I remembered how I'd felt, the first time I saw Caroline. Thrust back, abruptly, into the role of the outsider simply because Caroline looked so much like Louise, while all my life I'd sought, in vain, some resemblance to *anyone*. Then I remembered Louise the last time I saw her, laid out in her coffin, looking like no one, not even herself, gone from me totally.

229

I stared at Josefine, and the features we shared failed to lessen the feeling of strangeness.

That's how my thoughts skittered, trying to hear and not to hear Josefine's story of my conception and birth and her decision to place me for adoption.

"It was so hard just to live. We changed, all of us. We looked, if you can understand, for the best . . . how is it? For the best deal.

"The soldiers were everywhere. Your father was so handsome. . . .

"I always was a fool for a handsome man. That's the reason for your half-sister, Brigitte. She was five years old when you were born, and she used to feed you, but I think she was always jealous. . . .

"When Ernest was transferred back to the States, the support money he'd been giving went home with him. And when it became possible to see you in a good home with a good family, there was never any question. I believed what we all believed, that Americans were all rich, that the good life was there, in America, and that you'd have everything you could want in your life with a family like the McMillons.

"But now you tell me how you were mistreated. Dear God, how could I know? I was so sure I'd done the best thing for you, sending you to America."

We visited all the places that had figured in my beginnings, but nothing was the same, of course, not after thirty years. The hospital where I was born had been razed to the ground. The home where I'd stayed before my adoption was now a kindergarten. A car factory stood where Josefine had lived.

I don't know if I'd seriously expected anything different. I listened to her explanations about those days, long ago,

230

and felt remote—totally uninvolved. I tried to understand, not only what she was now—a respected secretary at a huge university in Munich—but also what she'd been like as little more than a girl.

She was twenty-one years old in 1949, and with her mother and Brigitte to support. Supplies were still short. Food was difficult to come by. It took the greatest ingenuity along with a fair smattering of luck to survive with any semblance of comfort.

I could understand that. Of course I could understand that.

The foreign troops filling the streets were a chance for that comfort. The Americans were noted for their kindness and generosity. Ernest Barnett, my father, was handsome and gentle, and Josefine fell for his line and went to bed with him. When she found out she was pregnant with me, her Catholic upbringing made abortion abhorrent. Yet Ernest would be going home quite soon, and the parting had always been accepted.

So she'd done the only thing her conscience would allow. She'd had me, then offered me for adoption.

It made good sense. Intellectually, not emotionally. I even tried to feel what she'd felt. Her utter desperation. I tried to have some sense of her as my mother, but I failed in this attempt. And one thought kept resurfacing no matter what she said.

She'd managed to keep her first daughter, Brigitte, the child of a French soldier. If I'd been white, like Brigitte, would she have managed to keep me as well?

"You were ashamed," I finally said, flatly, "because I was the child of a black soldier."

She looked at me for a long minute. She'd been crying over her memories. She stared at the soaked handkerchief in her hands, then put it carefully in her lap, and when she met my eyes again, hers never faltered. Her shoulders had gone

231

back and she was quite calm—she'd prepared herself for this one.

"I was never ashamed to have had you, Doris," she said simply. "But I was fully aware of the difficulties involved in trying to raise you here in Germany. I knew perfectly well what your life would be and how little you would be permitted to achieve. I knew what you would suffer in any relationships you tried to form, and how difficult, if not impossible, it would be for you to find a man when you were grown up.

"This is not to claim I was being totally without thought for myself."

She looked at me silently for a long second.

"You're a grown woman now. You have an understanding of what drives people to do what they do. I was still very young after you were born, and I was very beautiful."

This without embarrassment. In fact, she was studying me intently.

"I can see myself young when I look at you. You get your looks from me, Doris, though some credit has to go to Ernest, as well. He was fine-looking."

I think I smiled slightly.

"I was young and attractive, and I still had hopes for my own future. I didn't know then what I wanted that future to be, but I did know I couldn't *have* any decent future supporting my mother, myself, and two children. And with one of the children black, and in that environment . . ."

Her voice trailed off, and she stared back in time, and I felt her confusion and despair as a remote thing, recognized but not shared.

She was as open as she found it possible to be, yet the crux of my problem couldn't be gotten at with simple questions and filtered memories. What I'd hoped for, without fully realizing my focus, was a sense of instant familiarity.

I'd invested a lifetime of energy fantasizing this moment

232

with this woman as my confidante. I'd made her the perfect mother-image, the key to all the answers for all my personal insecurities. I'd wanted the unquestioned right to make Josefine understand the bitter anger and sense of rejection I'd suffered all my life. The aching loss that affected everything, though I'd never understood its true source or extent.

And I wanted the right to lash out at her now, to show her my feelings and try to work them through, and then to see and hear something of her own deepest emotions, too— but how could I? It was asking for an intimacy few people ever reach, and the fact of the blood tie meant nothing at all.

"Your sister, Brigitte, did not wish to come meet you," Josefine was musing. "I think, though it sounds ridiculous, that she has always been jealous of you because you had a complete family, and she didn't. She had only me." Josefine smiled, but her lips trembled. "What is it? The grass being greener . . . ?"

There was nothing I could say.

"Can you see that she might feel this way? That she would feel you'd been given a brand-new mother *and* father—she always felt her own lack of a father deeply. That you'd been given a new life in the golden land of America, while she had to remain here, and without any special benefits, certainly?"

"She knew, at least, that she was wanted," I said quietly, and it was Josefine's turn to let it pass unanswered.

After a bit, she continued, her hands clasped in her lap.

"And yet, she *is* your sister. I don't know what, if anything, you'll eventually want to do about meeting her, or if you'd prefer to leave things as they are. Time may make a difference. She may become accustomed again to the thought of you. To the fact that she's a grown woman, just as you are, married, as you are, with children. That jealousy at this point is ridiculous.

"The rest of the family greets you, though they didn't

know, most of them, I'd ever had a black child, and so you can imagine the stir it caused when I told them you were coming to see me."

The small group of strangers at the airport with Josefine had further strained an atmosphere already stretched thin. They'd been obviously embarrassed by the presence of the press, but I thought they'd been impressed by the coverage, too.

Josefine confirmed this.

"They liked the idea," she said, laughing, "that my daughter was a star on the American television."

A star. Me.

Josefine and I drew slowly closer as we compared all the shared things we despised or enjoyed. We both hated housework and especially cooking, unlike Louise, serene in her kitchen, chopping and stirring, more easygoing there than anyplace else I could recall. I hadn't remembered that small, happy picture in all the years of my adulthood.

"I'll never know how it all would have gone if I'd kept you," Josefine said one day. "If you would have grown up happier, even without the same opportunities. Maybe happiness should be the only consideration."

But I was realizing, finally, that she needed reassurance from *me,* too. Her eagerness to welcome me back after all the years had been rooted in more than natural mother-love. She'd felt guilt over the adoption, and this wasn't something she had to put into words, though she did. I could see and feel her guilt, and I'd intensified it greatly with my tales of childhood with Louise.

I couldn't imagine why I felt I owed her, just as I'd always felt she owed me, but the fact remained that I *did* feel that way, so I did my best, stating the obvious.

"Look at my life now," I said. "At all I have. At my potential, in my career. At whatever makes me, too." I considered this myself. "If adversity's supposed to develop

234

character, then I shouldn't have any problems with my character for the rest of my life, should I?" I tried to smile at this, but she was watching me gravely, searching for the lie because of her guilt.

But it wasn't a lie. The stating of it, for the first time, made me aware of my own personal development to that point—something I'd taken for granted along the way as almost everybody else does. I'd never thought about how lucky or unlucky I was. I'd only thought about sadness and rejection and loss.

"If you'd kept me," I said flatly, "what would I be today? Who would I have married? And what could I look forward to in a career?"

"But being secure and happy . . ." her voice faded.

I stated my greatest truth. "I could never be happy if I wasn't free to achieve whatever I'm capable of doing and being."

My trip was drawing rapidly to an end. And I felt uneasy, itchy. After all, what questions had really been answered? For that matter, what exactly had I wanted all my life, while indulging in my fantasies, other than a convenient escape whenever life became troublesome? I'd told myself I wanted Josefine to enfold me, mother to daughter. But meeting her now, at thirty years of age, made any such relationship impossible. The most I could hope for with Josefine was the sort of friendship I'd felt developing with Mom after the surgery.

The trip to Munich wasn't nearly long enough to answer any important questions, but it did foment a growing need to sort out my deepest beliefs from mere self-delusions. And Josefine kept on throwing out small tidbits to add to the considerations.

"It was your mother, Mrs. McMillon," she commented one evening, "who had determined to adopt a child. Not that she actually said this to me, you understand. It was Mr.

235

McMillon, your father, who told me this to impress on me how very much his wife would love my little girl."

I'd never once wondered which of them, Mom or Dad, had initiated the decision to adopt me. If I had thought of it, I suppose I would have thought it was Dad, wanting a child even if Louise couldn't give one to him.

Josefine looked back to that time, sighed, and shook her head.

"Mr. McMillon, himself, was excited, and trying to hold it all in. I'm sure he thought he was being so very calm and assured, you know." She smiled. "But he would not sit and seemed unable to wait and also talked quite a lot, and I had the impression that this was not his normal behavior."

I tried to picture this scene. Tried to tie it to an infant child—me. Could do so only as a mental exercise, feeling nothing real.

Josefine saw this. I found, quite early in my stay, that we thought along the same lines. We shared thoughts, in much the same way as Margaret and I did. We finished each other's sentences with ease and were nearly always in tune with one another's feelings.

It was very pleasant and a relief, but it wasn't "family."

"You've always expected too much out of this meeting, haven't you, Doris?" Josefine asked me quietly, as we finished up our last dinner together the night before my flight home to New York.

"Am I a very great disappointment?"

There was genuine curiosity in her voice, and a glint of amusement as she watched me.

I studied her in silence. Physically, she was so totally different than I'd dreamed. Even the fact that I looked so much like her was different than I'd ever allowed myself to believe. But in every other way . . . ?

"No," I said, having carefully considered it. "You're all the good, warm things I dreamed about as a child. The things I stopped letting myself believe you'd be when I was grown up and starting to be cynical about life." I grinned. "You know, that deep stuff.

"But you don't have my answers for me," I added honestly.

As usual, she understood this, too.

"You always had your own answers, Doris. And now that you don't have to be afraid of your background anymore, you'll loosen up enough to allow yourself to find them."

My answers? I tried to pull my *questions* all together on the flight home, but there was nothing clear enough to list as a question; there were just feelings, much harder to define. I didn't know if this meeting would magically erase the sense of rejection I'd nurtured all my life. But at least the obsession to find my natural mother had finally been faced and dealt with and was ended.

"You have two daughters of your husband's," Josefine had said right before I left her. "When are you planning to have a child of your own?"

I had no answer for her.

I had a lot of soul-searching still to get through. I somehow had to make the jump, holding all these new cards, from emotional insecurity to womanhood.

And I meant to find Ernest Barnett. That would close the circle for good.

I thought a lot about my trip once I was home. I found I couldn't talk about it to anyone except Raphael. Oh, the slick parts were easy, like an interview with the *New York Post* in which I gave all the set answers about the thrill of tracking down my natural mother: "It was wonderful. All I could do was look at her."

But alone, inside my head, truth came harder. "Real" and "unreal" had done a reverse. For I'd always thought of

237

Josefine in terms of my "real" mother. I'd resented the unknown Caroline all my life because she was Louise's "real" daughter. And I'd carried that deadly theme along, into marriage, viewing myself as just a poor substitute parent for Raphael's first wife, Martine, who was his daughters' "real" mother.

When Josefine stepped into my life, it was in the role of possible friend. There was nothing of mother-daughter in our relationship. It was true that we shared preferences for many things. We had a basis for hours and days of comfortable companionship. But the memories and shared joy and grief of a lifetime were missing with Josefine. All my memories were of, and with, my mom—Louise Evelyn.

Now, with my fantasy realized, I saw clearly that nothing was conveniently black or white. Every aspect of my early family life was a mixed blessing. My adoption, though it gave me to Louise, blessed me with Dad and his values. My childhood, with its emotional scars, drove me to succeed with my career and with my own marriage and children. Even the reunion with Josefine, my ultimate goal for so long, had its highs and lows. The obsession was satisfied, but the solutions to my emotional problems weren't in Munich. They were inside myself.

Mine wasn't a good childhood, and nothing would change that. But the problems were Mom's problems and had little to do with anybody else. The albums Mr. Murphy sent me had freed dormant thoughts. All the anger and hysteria stepped back, just a little, to make way for some better moments.

Like our shopping trips. The memory wasn't for the clothing, which was gone so quickly anyway, but for the laughter and sharing of preferences and taste, and the happiness of those hours we'd spent together.

More hours in the kitchen, learning how to cook. The patience Mom had shown, never getting irritated by my

238

endless questions, as long as they avoided adoption and Josefine. She was short on praise for any achievement, yes, even at the stove. But she *was* there beside me—something I'd taken very much for granted and then forgotten entirely in the cloud of misery that followed.

The night talks. She wasn't selective in her topics, and she'd seemed obsessed with sex and her bitterness toward men after she left Dad. She'd drummed her opinions into me, but she'd joked a lot, too, sometimes caustically, and all in all they were good times, those evenings with one soft lamp lit, and rain on the window, and the feel of the warm, soft quilt.

I remembered all the times of childhood sickness, too. All the step running, the efforts to divert me from a child's feverish misery. The hours spent beside my bed, her face calm and sure. I'd felt such utter security, then, knowing I couldn't possibly get sicker, that she wouldn't allow it—she was my mother.

Once these memories of a lifetime started to peek past the anger and resentment I'd nurtured for years, a whole tide of similar memories overwhelmed me. For the first time, I saw the *whole* of my life with Mom in context—the good and the terrible.

She'd been afraid. Yes. Dad was right. Of losing things, so she'd pushed them away—her *own* choice, then—before *she* could be rejected.

But she'd acted and reacted out of confusion, mental illness, and fear. Her love drove her to extremes, to protect herself from her own devils.

Her love drove her. For Dad and for me.

POSTSCRIPT

JOSEFINE CALLED ME SHORTLY after my return to New York. Our story was big news in Munich; the newspapers were still carrying it. An old acquaintance of Ernest Barnett's had seen the story and had written to Josefine with Barnett's current address.

He was living in New Jersey.

Right in my WABC viewing area.

I couldn't call him after all. In the end, Raphael did it for me. Barnett agreed to meet me, though he didn't sound overjoyed. And suddenly, antagonism, a sharp and twisting anger I hadn't felt for Josefine, focused on my natural father who'd left me without a thought.

Ernie-boy.

"You probably won't believe this." Barnett looked at me out of the corner of his eye, a middle-aged man totally unlike the pictures I'd recently been studying.

"I was thinking about you just this Thanksgiving."

I was silent. It didn't matter whether I believed him or not. I didn't *know* what I believed. All that mattered was finally closing the circle on my beginnings.

"I was with a bunch of my buddies, talking about the things that happened when we were younger. A lot of them had their families with them—it was a dinner reunion, you see? A lot of them had married girls when they were stationed in Germany, like me."

He shot me another glance, but I still said nothing. I couldn't think of anything to say. Far more than Josefine had been, my father was a stranger.

"There were some kids there, too. Kids from those marriages. I looked at them and I felt alone." He rubbed at his cheek with his fingertips, then covered his mouth with his hand and regarded me over his fist.

"I started wondering how you'd turned out. My little girl. How it would have been if I'd brought you back to the States with me when I was transferred home. If I'd raised you myself. My mother, she would have helped."

He seemed to think about that for a bit.

"I don't know," he finally admitted, shaking his head.

I roused myself from dark thoughts and made an effort. After all, this meeting was at my request.

"But it never came up, did it?" I asked, trying to keep my voice level. My anger was ridiculous—I couldn't let myself place the blame for a lifetime of insecurity on Ernest Barnett. He'd never even lived in my fantasy. He'd never been important enough. I'd never considered anyone but Horace McMillon my dad.

I didn't need a villain, did I? There were no villains in this story.

"It would have been real hard," he murmured. "But I wish I'd been stronger, considering it."

"Why didn't you bring Josefine and me back together?" I

244

asked the obvious, considering his little story of the reunion.

"Marry Josefine?" he said, his voice bewildered. He rubbed again at his mouth, then sighed. "I don't know," he shrugged. "I don't think Josefine and I ever really considered it."

And that was that. It didn't leave a whole lot to say. Not about all those years ago, in Munich, in the dead past. I made one brief effort to imagine it—a family composed of Josefine, Barnett, and myself. Couldn't do it. It seemed absurd.

"Didn't you see me on the news?" I finally asked him the question that was rubbing me raw. "Didn't you watch the station following my trip to Germany and my meeting with Josefine? Didn't you hear me ask for you, for news of Ernest Barnett, after I got back?"

He stared at me blankly.

"Afraid not, Doris," he finally said. "I don't watch your station."

I wasn't comfortable with Barnett. There were great long silences full of things he couldn't or wouldn't tell me, and even later, weeks later, in telephone calls, I felt no easier. And I wasn't sure he even mattered at all, for my thoughts were still on Josefine, back in Germany.

I kept thinking about what she'd told me about having to give me up. She'd needed a new start, but what had she made of that start? She never had married or had other children. She said she'd done it for my own good—sending me to America where everyone was rich. She said she'd suffered with the guilt of wondering if that choice was correct, and her suffering *was* obvious and should have been enough proof of love.

But regardless of her motives and feelings and doubts, I had to put it behind me now, all these elements of fact and fantasy. The problem was, I now had two new parents—strangers. I didn't have the slightest idea what to do about them. I couldn't just put them back out of my life, and I didn't yet know how to deal with them.

Surprise, surprise. I'd done it to myself again. I'd given myself a whole new set of potential problems. Two lives. People no longer young, and accepting me back as their adult child. Wanting the privileges of parenthood now, without having earned them. Brought to this point by me alone. Two more people to make me vulnerable, if I could love them.

And I had to be sure never to let it hurt Dad. Never to let him think, even for a second, that anyone, through a mistake of heredity, could possibly matter to me as he mattered.

Had I grown enough to take the chance on new relationships, while maintaining the old?

I didn't know. Time would test it. That was the only certainty.

One question *had* been answered by my finding Barnett and Josefine—the meaning of "real" in terms of family relationships. Manushka and Natasha weren't just *Raphael's* daughters, they were my daughters too. My real daughters. *I* was their real mother, now, the mother who would raise them from this point on. The mother who'd be sharing all the facets of their growing up. That's what "real" was.

I liked to think I'd do a better job than Mom had with me. That when my girls were women in their own right, they'd look back on childhood with warmth, not the chill bitterness I'd always felt. That the good things would come immediately to mind, and whatever my failings as their mother and their friend, these wouldn't be uppermost as concerns.

But that's in the future. Day-to-day manages most

246

things. Like remembering, no matter what the provocation, to give myself those vital seconds to think before saying hurtful, ugly things. Children remember when their parents are miserable.

And never allowing distinctions. Never. Not even in my own head. Never to distinguish between stepdaughters and a child of my flesh.

I was pregnant.

The real test of my growing up was just ahead.